PUB WAl
IN EAST SU

Forty Circular Walks

Around East Sussex Inns

Mike Power

Other publications in the series

"Pub Walks in Dorset"
"Forty More Pub Walks in Dorset"
"Pub Walks in Hampshire & the I.O.W."
"Pub Walks in West Sussex"
"Pub Walks in Devon"
"Pub Walks in Cornwall"
"Pub Walks in the New Forest"
"Pub Walks in Somerset"
"Pub Walks in North Surrey"
"Pub Walks in Hardy's Wessex"
"Pub Walks in Kent"
"Pub Walks in South Surrey"
"Pub Walks along the Dorset Coast"

1st edition published September 1994
Updated edition published April 2003

© **Power Publications**
1 Clayford Ave
Ferndown
Dorset. BH22 9PQ
E.mail: Sales@powerpublications.co.uk

ISBN 1898073 29 5

Publishers note
Whilst every care is taken to ensure that all the information given in this
book is correct, errors may occur due to many factors. Paths can be re-routed, stiles can
replace gates etc. etc. The pubs themselves change hands on a regular basis. Neither the
publishers nor the printers can accept responsibility for any inaccuracies.

Front cover: The Tiger Inn, East Dean
Printed by Pardy & Son (Printers) Ltd., Ringwood, Hampshire.

Introduction

Four years after writing 'Pub Walks in West Sussex', I have finally completed this companion book. Many memorable hours were spent exploring the villages, visiting the towns and the coast, walking across miles of beautiful countryside and discovering some great pubs the majority of which I have been able to include in this book. Most of them are well off the beaten track in idyllic village settings which I have chosen purely for their charm or vicinity to an interesting walk, no charge is made for inclusion in the book.

The walks are all circular, vary in length from $1\frac{1}{2}$ miles to $4\frac{3}{4}$ miles and are explained in detail with an accompanying sketch map. They are deliberately short to appeal to families and first time walkers and although planned to start and finish at the pub there is of course nothing to prevent you from starting anywhere along the route happy in the knowledge that refreshment is assured at some point. As a general guide allow 2 miles per hour. Parking can sometimes be a problem, but it is assumed you will want to return to the pub to sample their hospitality, on the rare occasion you may not I would respectfully ask you not to use their car park; where possible I have indicated suitable alternatives.

I am often asked where one can go to see the best display of bluebells as a guide there are woods on the following walks. No's 8, 11, 17, 26, 27, 30, 35, and 38. To help you the reference quoted at the start of each walk refers to the 1:50 000 - $1\frac{1}{4}$ inch to the mile in the Landranger series. It is always a good idea to have the appropriate map with you. The four you would need to cover these walks are No's 188, 189, 198 and 199.

Whilst many of the footpaths in the county are in reasonable condition sadly many are not. I know the County Council are working hard within their limited resources to open all paths but it could be a number of years yet before completion. Wherever I encountered a problem I have written to the authorities and hopefully by the time of publication they will have been attended to but if not you may have to pay particular attention to my instructions.

The new "Rights of Way Act" which came into force on August 13th 1990 has much improved the rights of ramblers; it is a massive step forward in path protection. The act now requires occupiers who disturb the land to make good the surface within 24 hours of the disturbance or two weeks if the disturbance is the first one for a particular crop. Where no width is recorded the minimum width of a path must now be one metre and two metres for a bridleway and the exact line of the path must be apparent on the ground. You are entitled to remove any obstruction but not to cause damage. If there is no way through you are entitled to leave the path and find an alternative route. Any problems you find should be reported to the county engineer in the rights of way section at Sackfield House in Lewes.

It has now been proved that walking is extremely good for you it can also be safe providing a few simple rules are observed. Wear suitable clothing; light weight quick drying or waterproof trouser are advisable as many paths become over-grown in summer. A waterproof jacket or cagoule is an essential item so too are strong waterproof boots but any comfortable footwear is alright provided it is well treaded. Take care on lanes without pavements and always walk facing the oncoming traffic, except on a dangerous right-hand bend. A compass can be useful so too can a torch if you are walking in the late evening. I always carry a stick it is ideal for clearing brambles, testing wet ground and can be waived in the air to deter frisky animals.

Wherever you go always remember the country code. Guard against all fires. Fasten gates. Keep dogs under control and always on a lead where there are livestock. Keep to the path across farm land. Take all litter home. Respect wild life and do not pick wild flowers. I very much enjoyed all these walks and the hospitality of the pubs I hope you will too.

Mike Power

EAST SUSSEX

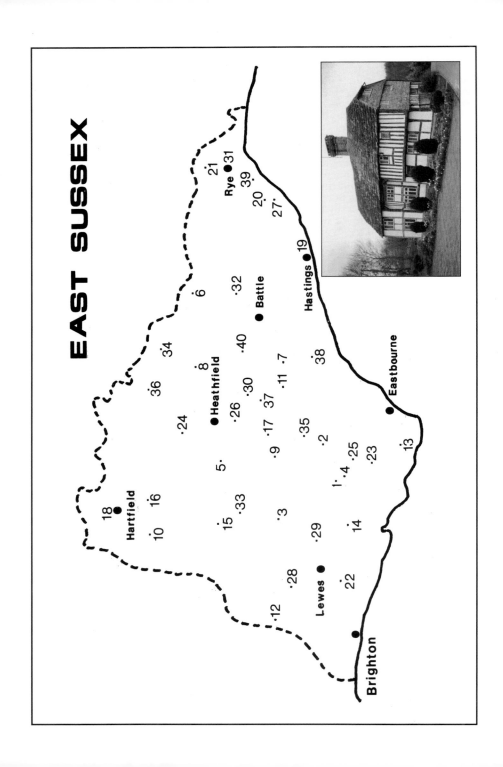

·21
Rye ●31
·39
·20
·27

·6
·32

Battle ●

Hastings ●19

·34
·40

·8
·36
Heathfield ●
·26 ·30
·17 ·37 ·11 ·7

·38

·24

·5·
·9
·35
·2

·1· ·4 ·25
·23

Eastbourne ●

·13

18 ●
Hartfield
·10 ·16
·15 ·33
·3

·29
·14

·28
Lewes ●
·22

·12

Brighton ●

Rose Cottage Inn, Alciston

Timeless Alciston village lies immediately under a spur of Firle Beacon, many very attractive dwellings line the one main street and the tithe barn, part of Alciston Court, is said to be the largest in the country. Beyond the wisteria draped exterior of Rose Cottage a relaxed atmosphere pervades in the main bar which has simple pew style seating, old prints, farm implements and stuffed birds decorating the part panelled walls and an old Victorian fireplace housing a warm log fire in winter. A small beamed area at the bar, presided over by Jasper an African grey parrot, leads through to a very attractive and cosy, low beamed dining room with a large inglenook fireplace with more seating in an adjoining room. There are picnic benches on the sunny front terrace and many old enamelled advertising signs fixed to the back fence.

The inn is a freehouse very well run by the owners Tan and Ginny Lewie. On offer is a good range of house wines and a couple of real ales from W J King & Co., Horsham Best Bitter and Red River.

A comprehensive bar menu, available seven days a week 12–2 and 7–9.30 (9 Sunday) which includes homemade soup and ploughman's, is supplemented by daily blackboard specials such as steak and kidney pudding, Thai chicken curry and chicken Neapolitan - mushrooms, tomatoes and herbs with grilled cheese. Vegetarians have a choice of dishes like Stilton and leek quiche and filo baskets with mushrooms, red wine and sour cream. Fresh fish is a speciality, which on my last visit included whole sea bass, marinated in ginger and soy sauce and grilled whole plaice with lemon and parsley butter. The evening bar menu offers additional items such as smoked salmon cornets filled with prawns and half a roast Sussex duckling served with a sauce of orange and green peppercorns.

Families are welcome but no children under 10. There is no objection to well behaved dogs.

Weekday opening times 11.30–and 6.30–11.

Telephone: 01323 870377

Village is just south of the A27 between Lewes and Polegate.

Approx. distance of walk: 4 miles. O.S Map No 199 TQ 506/057.

Park behind the pub or in the lane at the front.

One of my favourite downland walks especially for the spring time display of wild flowers. It is very scenic, not too arduous and mostly good underfoot except for the field paths which are often wet in winter. For a longer walk you could combine this walk with the walk from Berwick on page 12.

1. Leave the pub turning left walking back down the lane until you reach a small track leading to a stile on the left opposite house No 53. Go over into the field and across in the direction of the waymark making for the stile and plank bridge opposite, then continue ahead into the field ignoring the stile on the left. Keeping close to the hedge walk round and down the field to the stile at the bottom, up to the stile at the top, out into the lane and turn left.

2. In fifty paces turn right onto the signed bridleway leading to the pottery. After easy walking on a concrete surface the path enters a field. Maintain your direction to the open gateway and into the field ahead making for the hedge on the far side soon to reach the gate turning left onto the drive.

3. Bear right at the farm, past the barn and across the track following the bridleway it as it rises gradually up to a small wooden gate. Pass through onto the downs and turn left to join the sunken track up the hillside occasionally taking time to look back and enjoy the view and glance around the ground where many cowslips and other wild flowers can be seen carpeting the hillside in spring. Although not over steep it can be quite a puff to the top. Pass thorough the gate turning left at the finger post onto the South Downs Way.

4. On a clear day you have a lovely panoramic view. Upon reaching Bo Peep Bostal turn left following the lane down between the downs until you reach the sharp left-hand bend. On the right is a gate go through and turn left down between the trees soon to reach a stile on the left. Descend the steps following the deep, shaded, wild flower lined path down into the field and onto the track turning right eventually entering the village returning to the pub.

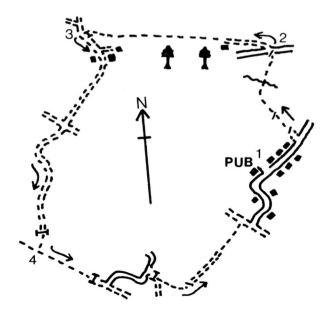

Yew Tree Inn, Arlington

Arlington, although only minutes from the busy A27 and a short drive from Eastbourne, is as peaceful a village as you will find anywhere in the County. At its centre and close to the ancient church is the rustic Yew Tree, a delightful country inn adorned with climbing plants and colourful flower baskets. It is a particular favourite with families in the summer for its very good children's play area and a small paddock with farm animals. On my last visit children were enjoying the thrill of hand feeding orphan lambs.

There are two bars in this cottage inn, the simply furnished, part panelled and bare boarded public bar heated by an open log fire in winter, and the more comfortable and relaxing carpeted saloon. At the back is a pretty dining area with a large unusual brick fireplace and patio doors leading out onto the terrace and rear back lawn with randomly placed white tables and chairs.

The inn is a freehouse lovingly run by the long-standing owner Peter Laws. There are usually a couple of real ales such as the local Harvey's plus Carling, Stella and Grolsch.

Popular home-cooked bar food, served daily 12–2 and 6–9, Saturday and Sunday all day 12–9 and listed on the blackboard might include soups, garlic mushrooms and deep fried Camembert followed by a choice of roasts, homemade steak and kidney pie, baked mushroom roly poly, breast of chicken with a Stilton sauce, bacon and onion pudding and king prawn platter. Specials might include salmon, vegetarian tortilla, pasta, crespelle and many others whilst sweets range from After Eight mint gateau and lemon lush butterscotch calypso to treacle sponge pudding and apple mincemeat pie.

Children and dogs equally welcome.

Weekday opening times 11–3 and 6–11 Sunday all day 12–10.30.

Telephone: 01323 870590.

Village signed north from the A27, 3 miles west of Polegate.

Approx. distance of walk: 4¼ miles O.S Map No 199 TQ 544/074.

Park in the pub's own car park, outside in the lane or in the car park opposite the church.

A most enjoyable but fairly challenging walk especially when the weather is bad then waterproof footwear is essential. The route at first follows a footpath close to the Cuckmere River before reaching a pretty bridleway leading into Nate and Abbots Wood returning across farm land.

1. Turn right from the pub into the lane leading to the church and cross the stile into the field. Bearing half left make your way across to the stile and plank bridge, enter the field and keep straight ahead to the stile opposite. Maintaining direction make for the corner of the dwelling, walk up to the stile, out onto the drive and keep straight ahead soon to turn left into the lane.

2. At the bend in the road keep straight ahead onto the signed footpath. It is a wide grass track with many springtime wild flowers along its length notably cuckooflowers and primroses. Dry at first it can soon become extremely muddy only negotiable with care in very bad weather. Walk until the track divides then fork left, cross the stream and then fork right. The track soon merges with a tarred lane and reaches the road.

3. Walk up the hill and on the bend turn left into Robin Post Lane. After entering Nate Wood on the gravel track continue walking until you reach a cross track then turn left, Further ahead fork right following the main but often muddy track eventually reaching the junction of several paths. Take the one on the left signed, to The Car Park. If you have brought some refreshment with you there are several picnic benches when you reach Plackett Coppice. Thereafter follow the main drive out of the car park, up to the road and turn left.

4. On the right opposite the Polegate turning is a stile. Go into the field, then over the stiles on the left turning right. More stiles lead you around the edge of a small-holding and into a large field. Keeping to the hedge on the right walk round until you reach the pair of stiles and plank bridge on the right, Cross into the field and bear half left making for the pair of stiles in the far hedge. Maintain your direction close to the pylon and leave by the stile, crossing the lane onto the signed footpath opposite. walk down beside the house to the stile and plank bridge, bear right in the field in the direction of the church, leave by the gate up the path to the pub.

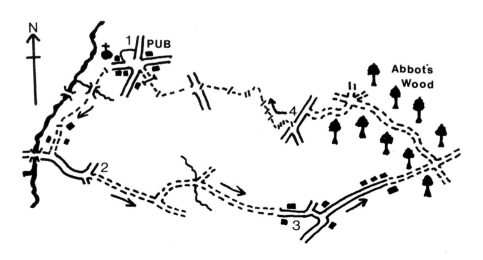

The Anchor Inn, Barcombe

The remotely situated and picturesque Anchor Inn lies at the end of a long peaceful lane beside the River Ouse. Sadly in 1994 and again a couple of years ago, the rising waters of the Ouse partly submerged the pub after which very extensive repair work was necessary to every room. Whilst the one small cosy bar was being redecorated a second bar was added. It has a beamed ceiling and a stove in one alcove. There is a separate family room with a guarded open fire and an attractive candle lit restaurant decorated in the traditional manner – both rooms are non-smoking. Those seeking relaxation will find no better spot than the newly landscaped front beer garden beside the river but the more adventurous can hire a boat. The inn has a marriage license for the those couples wanting a different sort of day.

The inn is a friendly freehouse well run by Carl the manager. The well stocked bar includes three real ales, Badger Best, Harvey's Best Biter and the light golden Tanglefoot plus local Longford wine.

Very good food, all home cooked on the premises, is available seven days a week Monday to Friday 12–3 and 6–9.30, Saturday and Sunday all day 12–9.30. Apart from the bar menu which lists the usual snacks like sandwiches, ploughman's and jacket potatoes wider tastes are catered for. There is usually an interesting homemade soup such as Stilton and broccoli followed by fresh fish which might include sea bass, mussels or monkfish. Further blackboard specials might include pork, capers and apple pie, beef and stout casserole, steak with a Roquefort sauce plus a vegetarian dish. Half price meals are available for children but there are no chips.

On weekdays, from June through till mid September, the pub is open all day from 11–11 but usually closes between 3 and 6.30 in the winter depending on trade.

There are three double rooms for those seeking overnight accommodation. Two more added at the end of 2002.

Telephone: 01273 400414.

Not the easiest pub to find although it is well signed. Situated north of Lewes, Barcombe Cross can be reached from both the A275 and the A26 the latter being the better route. Having entered the village continue north and take the right turn just before reaching Mount Pleasant.

Approx. distance of walk: 3½ miles O.S.Map No.198 TQ 443/161.

Park at the front or in the field opposite.

A very enjoyable walk ideal for a summers day. The first half is along the banks of the Ouse then through woods on a wide track before returning across farm land and along a peaceful country lane. Whilst fairly flat and easy going the walk can sometimes be quite muddy in the winter.

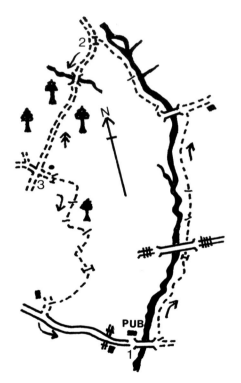

1. Turn left from the pub and cross the river soon to climb the stile on the left onto the riverside path following it round to the gate. Go under the old railway bridge and continue following the path over a couple of stiles until you eventually reach the track. Turn left, cross the bridge and immediately climb the stile on the right to join the riverside path. Further round cross the stile and continue walking finally to reach the farm gate leading out onto the track and turn left.

2. After crossing the Longford Stream the track enters woodland. Although extensively felled and coppiced some tall handsome fir trees still remain above an attractive ground carpet of wild flowers including bluebells, white wood anemones and primroses. Continue walking for about half a mile uphill to a cross track.

3. Close to a pond on the left is a stile beside a gate. Go over into the field and walk straight ahead making your way up to the finger post then turn right skirting the woods. Cross the stile ahead of you turning left at the next stile and follow the path round the headland beside the bluebell wood. Climb the stile and plank bridge into the field on the left then turn right. At the next stile go over into the field on the right and bear half left, down to the gate way then up towards the farm buildings. Leave by the stile, turn left through the farm yard, into the lane and left again back to the pub, a distance of just over half a mile.

The Cricketers Arms, Berwick

Although very close to the busy A27 Berwick is as peaceful a village as you might find anywhere in rural Sussex. Voted 'Sussex Pub of the Year' 1997, the delightful Cricketers Arms, built some 500 years ago, has only been a pub for about the last 200, and most of that time in the same family. Customers can relax outside in the beautiful, shrub and flower filled garden or in one of three attractive rooms. The middle bar, the original pub, has part panelled walls, a red brick floor and heated by an open fire in winter. The end room, a perfectly matched extension, is ideal for walkers being simply furnished but the most atmospheric room, originally the owners living quarters, is now an attractive bar having a low beamed ceiling, rustic furniture and a warm log fire in a raised hearth.

The inn is owned by Harvey's, beautifully kept and well run by the licensee Peter Brown. Well kept Harvey's Best is still served traditionally straight from the cask with an additional beer such as Old in the winter.

Tasty bar food is served all week winter 12–2.15 and 6.30–9, summer 12–9.30, weekends all day 12–9, the majority cooked locally on the premises from ingredients direct from Convent Garden and local suppliers. Daily specials such as smoked haddock mornay, roasted vegetables, feta cheese quiche and game pie supplement the bar menu where there is a choice of homemade soup, pate, various ploughman's, filled jacket potatoes and filled 'Vienna' rolls. In addition you could choose a prime T-bone steak, local pork and chive sausages, home-baked ham with egg and chunky chips, a vegetarian special and 'Cricketers' selection–breaded Japanese prawns, scampi and plaice goujons. Puddings listed include treacle sponge, homemade fresh fruit crumble and passion fruit sorbet.

Weekday opening times are from 11–3 and 6–11. All day summer and weekends. Families are welcome but children restricted, dogs inside and out.

Telephone: 01323 870469. Fax: 871411. www.cricketersberwick.co.uk

Village signed south from the A27 between Lewes and Polegate.

Approx. distance of walk: 2¾ miles. O.S.Map No.199 TQ 519/052.

Park at the pub or in the lane at the front.

A very enjoyable, mostly level, family walk ideal for a summers day. Although fairly good underfoot during periods of extremely wet weather some of the bridleways can be deep in mud. For a longer walk you could combine this one with the walk from Alciston on page 6.

1. Leave the pub and turn right, walk to the top of the village, round to the right keeping straight ahead onto the concrete farm road and enter the field. Make your way across to the far side on the raised path turning left when you reach the hedge. Ignore the footpath on the right but keep walking shortly to reach the raised track then turn left.
2. Cross the junction of the two bridleways to eventually reach the dwelling then turn left onto the grassy path down between the fields. At the bottom turn left onto the cross track following it round, and down to meet the road then turn left.

3. Carefully follow the road for about a quarter of a mile and just before reaching Drusillas Park look for the signed bridleway on the left. Appealing to all ages this famous zoo was the winner in "Englands Family Welcome of the Year". It is a fairly wide but sometimes muddy grass track dotted with many different wild flowers along its length. After entering the field head towards the church turning right just before the gate. Cross the stile into the field and bear slightly left over to the stile in the far fence. Walk between the buildings skirting the pond back to the pub.

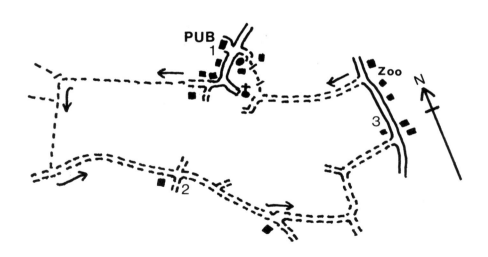

The sketch maps in this book are not necessarily to scale but have been drawn to show the maximum amount of detail.

The Blackboys Inn, Blackboys

It was a sad day indeed when fire devastated the beautiful Blackboys Inn but after months of careful restoration, happily it is now back to its former glory. Inside this ancient 14th century pub is an excellent bare boarded public bar, simply furnished with extra seating in the lovely inglenook fireplace. The attractive, panelled main bar has exposed beams, wood parquet flooring and comfortable window seats, whilst three inter-connected rooms (two of which are non-smoking) provide a comfortable ambience for diners. Outside there are benches positioned on the front green, in the garden area and on the patio surrounding the newly refurbished large duck pond.

The inn is owned by Harvey's and extremely well run by amiable tenants, Edward and Claire Molesworth. The complete range of Harvey's ales are stocked plus cask conditioned cider and a good range of wines.

The menu is available seven days a week, with the exception of Sunday evening, and there are daily specials chalked on the blackboards. The bar snack menu includes homemade soup, ploughman's, homemade steak, kidney and ale pie, seafood pancake, ham and chips and a very popular steak 'butty'. The à la carte menu offers dishes such as baked haddock served with a saffron and basil vinaigrette, new potatoes, vine ripened cherry tomatoes and French green beans, also breast of chicken stuffed with roasted Mediterranean vegetables served on boulangere potatoes with a duo of vinaigrettes, Thai tuna salad and pan fried fillet steak with a mushroom, cream and brandy sauce served with sauté potatoes and seasonal vegetables. There are also several vegetarian dishes available including open cap mushrooms with oven roasted tomatoes and goats cheese, vegetarian gallette and Mediterranean tartlets served with bread and salad.

Weekday and Saturday opening times are from 11–3 and 6–11, Sunday 12–3 and 7–10.30.

Well behaved children are welcome in the dining rooms, dogs in the bar areas. Telephone: 01825 890283.

Pub sited back from the road on the B2192 west of Heathfield.

Approx. distance of walk: 4¼ miles. O.S.Map No. 199 TQ 522/204.

Park at the front of the pub or in School Lane at the side.

An enjoyable country walk exploring field paths, peaceful country lanes and sections of both the Wealdway and the Vanguard Way. Whilst a mostly level walk and good underfoot some areas can be quite muddy after rain.

1. Leave the pub and turn left into School Lane looking for a signed path part way up on the left almost opposite Green Close. Walk into the play area and turn right up the field and out into the road at the top. Cross to the stile opposite and follow the path through the allotments, out into the gravel road and turn left. Almost immediately take the signed footpath on the right. Climb the stile into the field and bear left walking round, and down to the hedge gap descending the slope to the farm gate turning right.

2. Walk past the house, cross the river and keep straight ahead up to the wooden gate by the cottage. Go through into the field and turn left onto the Weald Way. Cross the stiles and plank bridge turning right into the field making for the gate on the far side then bear left down the field to the stile, go out into the lane and turn left.

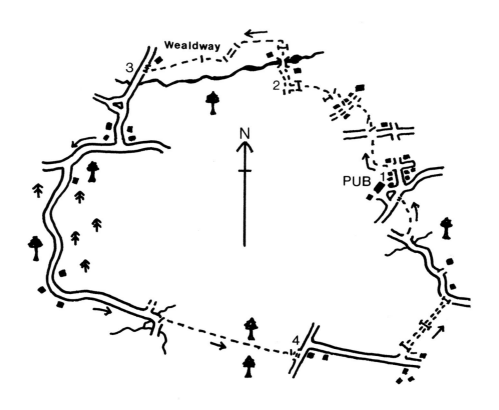

3. Bear left at the junction towards Black-boys then right into the road and further ahead cross over into Pump Lane, signed to Halland. Follow this peaceful and attractive lane through woodland for just under a mile. At the sharp right hand-bend, just beyond the gateway to Newplace Farm, cross the stile into the field on the left and head up the rise. At first keep fairly close to the hedge on the left then make for the gap in the trees ahead, walk through the gateway, up to the stile in the top hedge, down the steps into the lane and turn left.

4. In a hundred paces cross over into the lane opposite towards Waldron. Keep walking until you reach Vanguard Way the first track on the left, pass through the gate or cross the stile and follow it through a couple more gates, out into the lane and turn left. After crossing the river go into the field on the right, now managed by The Woodland Trust. Keep straight ahead to the stile then bear half left back up the field to the pub at the top.

Bodiam Castle

The Castle Inn, Bodiam

The pub is situated in a lovely position overlooking fields and within sight of the castle. Although the present Victorian pub was built on this site in 1885 it previously occupied a position on the opposite side of the road when it was known as the Red Lion. The mostly open plan interior consists of two rooms having part wood and part painted walls and a large brick fireplace housing an open log fire in winter. Furnishings are an assortment of chairs, various tables and a padded settle. There is a comfortable dining room and the pub has occasional live music. Outside there is a boules pitch and seating on the sunny back terrace with more on the lawn. Occasional live music.

This inn is now owned by Shepherd & Neame well run by the licensee Craig Wild. The brewery's full range of ales include Masterbrew, Spitfire and seasonal beers like Goldings Early bird plus a range of lagers.

Food times in the summer, all day at weekends flexible during the week, winter weekdays 12–2 and 7–9 but not Sunday evening. Apart from a good range of sandwiches, baked baguettes, salads and ploughman's, blackboard specials might include guinea fowl wrapped in bacon and stuffed with Applewood Cheddar with a red wine and wild mushroom sauce, savoury pancakes filled with spinach, Camembert and mushrooms topped with a tomato and garlic sauce and pan fried fresh tuna on a cherry tomato and onion salad with a balsamic vinegar and thyme dressing. The spring and summer menu lists traditional leek and potato soup, homemade steak and ale pie and pan fried lambs liver in bacon and onion gravy whilst the Sunday lunch menu offers four starters followed by two roasts, poached fillet of Highland salmon and buttered garlic penne pasta with button mushrooms, spinach and sun dried tomatoes.

Children and dogs both equally welcome inside and out.

Opening times: summer all day 11–11, Sunday 12–10.30, winter Monday–Thursday 11–3 and 6–11.

Telephone: 01580 830330.

Walk No. 6

Village signed from the A229 north of Hastings.

Approx. distance of walk: 2 miles. O.S.Map No 199 TQ 782/254.

The inn has its own car park alternatively you can use the National Trust park opposite. The current charge is 50p.

Although only a short walk at just over 2 miles it is nevertheless very enjoyable mostly across undulating farm land and through the grounds of Bodiam Castle. Completed in 1388 its outer walls and towers still stand today. Fortunately by that time the English had regained control of the channel and the castle was never attacked by the French.

1. Leave the pub and cross the road into the car park opposite then bear left following the path, through the gate walking round to the right of the castle. On the far side keep straight ahead up the grass to the stile in the hedge. It is to the right of the visitor centre where tickets can be obtained to enter the castle. The present charge is £2-50. It is open from April to the end of October between 10 a.m. and 6 p.m. November to March daily, except Monday from 10 a.m. till sunset.

2. Follow the Sussex Border Path up to the stile at the top, across to the next stile then straight ahead down to the stile in the wooden fence and enter the field. Walk down to the bottom and turn left following the hedge until you reach the stile on the right. Cross into the field and bear half left leaving by the gap in the bottom corner.

3. Turn right into the lane and then immediately left. Walk past the dwellings, and upon reaching the bend, go through the gate into the field on the left and bear left down to the plank bridge and gate. Bearing right climb the field to the stile in the fence then head straight across to the stile opposite, through the play ground, into the road, up to the junction and turn right. At the end of the cul-de-sac pass through the kissing gate on the left following the path up to the lane and turn right.

4. Cross over and immediately turn left into the lane leading to Newhouse Farm. The hedgerows are very attractive especially in early spring when there are lots of primroses in bloom. Keep walking until you reach the cross track then turn left. After negotiating one last crossing point beside a gate the track will eventually bring you straight back to the pub.

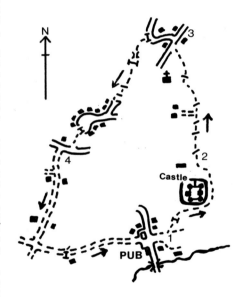

The White Horse Inn, Bodle Street Green

The present White Horse Inn was built about 1850 but the original pub, demolished all bar the cellar, was on a site fifty metres north now known as Brick House. Separated into two distinct areas, the bar is divided by a wooden screen and heated by an open fire in winter. Hanging on the walls are lots of old photographs. One of them, taken around the turn of the century, shows the landlord sat in a model T Ford outside the pub when it was owned by the Star Brewery. There are picnic benches on the sunny front, flower filled terrace and a helpful Ordnance Survey map is secured to the side wall. The pub is beautifully kept throughout, even the toilets are worthy of inspection. Folk night alternate Mondays.

Very well run and affectionately cared for by the owners Dave and Teresa Hosie the well stocked bar lists Harvey's Sussex Bitter plus a monthly guest ale, Stella, Carling, Guinness and Stowford Press cider.

Very good food is served every day 12–2 and 7–9. Individually cooked and prepared to order starters range from soup and mushrooms in hot garlic butter to deep-fried Camembert with cranberry sauce and California cocktail with taco bread. There is a traditional homemade steak and kidney pie, chilli, gammon steak, various curries, salads, smoked haddock pasta and summer Tahitian melon–half filled with prawns. A speciality seafood platter includes crevettes, king prawns, seafood sticks, prawns and salmon with a choice of dips. Vegetarians have a choice of five or six daily specials whilst sweet lovers can choose a particularly good banoffi pie made by Teresa. Separate children's menu.

Opening times 12–3 and 7–11 (Saturday 6.30)

Dogs in garden only children welcome if dining with parents.

Tel: 01323 833243.

Walk No. 7

Village signed north from the A271 at Windmill Hill.

Approx. distance of walk: 3 miles O.S.Map No 199 TQ 652/146.

Park either behind the inn, in the lane or in the Village Hall car park opposite.

An enjoyable walk which takes you along peaceful country lanes, follows the course of Christians River to Great Buckstepe, crosses open farm land and returns along an attractive bridleway close to Nunningham Stream. At the time of walking signing on some paths was nonexistent but I am confidently assured it is being attended to.

1. Leave the pub turning left into North Road. Beyond the houses, after just passing beneath the high electricity cables, enter the field through the metal farm gate on the left and cross to the gate opposite. Maintain your direction heading for the distant house then bear left up to the gate (unless the definitive route shown to the right of Water Mill Farm is now signed and accessible) and turn right onto the drive passing between the barn and the house. Just before reaching the bridge cross the grass on the left, go through the gate and into the meadow walking towards the house.

2. Upon reaching the boundary to Great Buckstepe Farm bear right, cross the stream and join the bridleway north around Great Buckstepe Farm following the driveway up to meet the lane. Keep straight ahead up the rise until you reach a gateway on the left signed to Thorneyfold Farm, now converted to a private dwelling (footpath marker stone on the right). Unless indicated to the contrary at some future date, walk down the drive to the gate in the wall, across the garden, into the field at the back and bear left over to the stile in the corner.

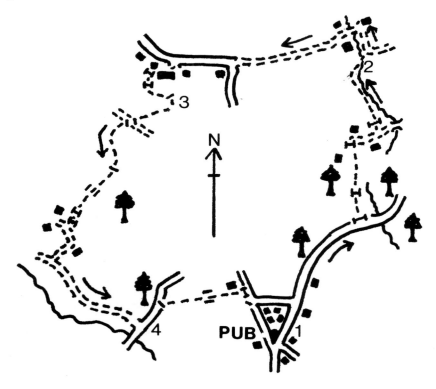

3. Keep straight ahead close to the field boundary, over the pair of stiles and then bear slightly to the left across the field making for the stile in the bottom hedge. Proceed to the gap in the hedge opposite and then across to the gates, out onto the track at Hole Farm turning left. Walk past the converted mill turning left onto the tarred drive soon to turn left again when you reach the lane.

4. An attractive mix of wild flowers including bluebells, cow parsley, pink campion and pearlwort compete for space in the quarter of a mile of hedgerows before you reach the stile on the right. Climb the bank and bear left across the field, through the open gateway and head for the right of the barn leaving by the stile or gate into the lane and turn right back to the pub.

Approaching Great Buckstepe

The Bell Inn, Burwash

The main bar of this lovely 17th century inn is simply but comfortably furnished, with a winter log fire and lots of interesting regalia displayed on the walls, which includes a collection of old barometers. The charming restaurant has a dark heavily beamed ceiling hung with interesting items and hop flowers. There is comfortable pew style seating on a carpeted floor and red bricks in front of the delightful corner fireplace.

Owned by Beards the pub is run by licensees Colin and Gillian Barrett together with their daughter and son-in-law. There is usually a choice of four real ales, which include two regulars, Marston's Pedigree and Morland Old Speckled Hen.

Food is served seven days a week but not Sunday evening. Warming winter soups with crusty bread, various platters, filled potatoes, pate, crispy coated garlic mushrooms, Japanese prawns and white bait etc. will head the snack list followed by dishes which might include grilled lamb cutlets, cauliflower cheese, homemade steak and kidney and chicken and mushroom pies, a seafood platter, home-cooked ham and eggs, pork steaks in a creamy mushroom sauce, cheese and broccoli quiche, hot n' spicy chicken breasts, chilli, lasagne, a good choice of vegetarian dishes and various other pasta dishes. And to complete your meal tempting traditional puddings like spotted dick, jam roly-poly and assorted gateaux.

Weekday opening times are from 11–3 and 5.30–11.

Children are welcome eating with parents, dogs in the bar on a lead.

Telephone: 01435 882304.

Village situated on the A265 about 6 miles east of Heathfield. The pub is opposite the church.

Approx. distance of walk: 2¾ miles O.S. Map No 199 TQ 677/247.

Parking is limited at the pub and restricted in the road at the front. There is however a little used free car park in the centre of the village.

A enjoyable walk which first takes you down a country lane and across farm land, then twice crosses the Rother, passes through a small but attractive bluebell wood before following a track back to the village. Nearby Bateman's, the home of Rudyard Kipling from 1902 until 1936, and where he wrote "Puck of Pook's Hill", is open daily 11 a.m. - 5 p.m. from April-October except Thursday and Friday

1. Leave the pub turning left then left again into Shrub Lane. In about three quarters of a mile look for a signed bridleway on the left leading to a farm. Pass through the gate following the track to the stile beside the gate at the back, walk down the field to the gate in the boundary, cross the stream and bear left in the direction of the bridge.

2. Go over into the field and bear right making for the boundary. Keep to the field edge, through the gateway into the field ahead and stay on the track as it bears left and then right before reaching a wooden post at which point turn left towards the bridge. Cross into the field and keep straight ahead up to the far hedge then turn left, pass through the gap and turn right. Walking beside the hedge arrive at the stile and plank bridge then bear half left to the stile on the edge of the wood.

3. In late spring the very attractive path snakes across a colourful carpet of bluebells, primroses and the occasional purple spotted orchid. Leave the wood by the stile and bear right up the field to the stile in the far hedge, cross over onto the track and turn right, pass through the gates and join the lane back up to the village turning left into the road back to the pub.

Key to Symbols

───── road	┄┄┄┄ track	┄┄┄┄ undefined path
✔ stile	⟩─⟨ bridge	├──┤ gate
┤ ├ gap in hedge	⊟ cattle grid	

Six Bells, Chiddingly

As a devotee of the traditional English pub I was delighted when I first visited the Six Bells at Chiddingly. On a raised level, the smaller bar, in this charming old fashioned hostelry, has a beamed ceiling, farmhouse tables, chairs and simple wooden settles. A pianola together with many rolls of music occupies one wall whilst stuffed animals and prints are displayed on the others. For cold mortals the massive step-in inglenook fireplace has seats at either end. The largest bar has a red brick floor and high back farmhouse chairs in front of the warm log fire. An assortment of interesting settles fit snugly into the secluded alcoves behind which is a lobby, where families are welcome, and an outside patio with seating. A separate adjoining barn style room, crammed to the roof with masses of old regalia and bric-a-brac, stages music at weekends.

Happily the pub is a freehouse well run by the licensees Paul and Jacqui Newman. At present there are two real ales, Director's Best and beautifully conditioned Harvey's Best Bitter served in time honoured tradition straight from the cask.

The pub is well known locally for its good reasonably priced bar food. Available weekdays 12–2.30 and 6–10.30, Saturday all day 12–10 and Sunday 12–9. On my last visit I noted carrot and coriander soup, a warm smoked chicken salad, garlic prawns, hot tuna and pasta bake, pigman's lunch with honey roast ham, and ploughman's lunch with Stilton. Also on the list was a cheesy vegetable bake, shepherds pie, ravioli in a spicy sauce, chicken and mushroom pizza, steak and kidney pie, spare ribs in barbecue sauce, spicy prawns Mexicana, chicken curry and filled jacket potatoes.

There is an area for children and dogs are allowed on a lead.

Weekday opening times 11–3 and 6–11, all day weekends. Bar open to midnight Friday, Saturday and Sunday.

Telephone: 01825 872227.

From the A22, 3 miles west from Hailsham, take the turning north at Golden Cross and then the next turning left at Muddles Green.

Approx. distance of walk: 2½ miles. O.S.Map No 199 TQ 544/142.

Ample parking is available either in the pub's own car park or the lane opposite but there is also a free car park by the church.

A very enjoyable walk mostly across farm land on well marked paths making it ideal for families. Although not over demanding it can be muddy in places during the winter.

1. Make your way from the pub into the lane opposite leading to the church and just beyond the telephone box pick up the signed footpath beside the dwelling. Cross the stile into the field and keep straight ahead to the stiles opposite. Continue ahead over the stile onto the wide grass path between the fields and after a series of stiles, turn right when you eventually reach the lane.

2. Almost immediately cross the stile on the left onto the narrow grass path. At the end climb the stile into the field maintaining direction through a couple of squeeze stiles, into an open field and across to the stile in the far hedge. Go out into the lane and turn left.

3. Proceed along this peaceful lane and after rounding the bend go through the farm gateway on the left onto the signed public footpath. Before reaching the farm take the stile in the fence on the left. Across the small field to the stile opposite to join the narrow path between the fields. Upon reaching the woods climb the fence and turn right following the path, round the bluebell wood, past the pond and up the bank into the field.

4. Turn left and continue walking towards the wooden crossing point. Go over into the field ahead and bearing slightly right, walk down to the concrete bridge, across into the field and up to the stile at the top. Cross over onto the track soon to turn left, through Friths Farm then left again into the lane. Ignore the turning for Horam but continue along the lane back to the pub.

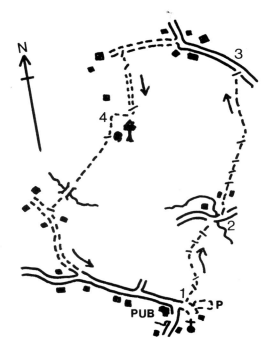

The Hatch Inn, Coleman's Hatch

The Hatch Inn was originally three cottages built in 1430, and did not become a public house until the 18th century, when it was given the name 'The Cock'. It wasn't until later that The Hatch acquired its present name to accommodate Colman's Hatch, meaning, gateway to the Royal Ashdown Forest. Situated at the bottom of Kid's Hill in the heart of the Forest it is just minutes away from the Pooh locations such as the famous Pooh Bridge. It is classed as a real 'locals pub' because of the warm and friendly atmosphere which is projected by the bar staff enhanced also by warm winter fires and candle lit tables. From the two beer gardens one has a good view of the beautiful surroundings.

Being a free house The Hatch Inn can always offer a range of quality beers which include those from Harvey's of Lewes and traditional Larkins ale plus other guests. The inn was commended in the CAMRA good beer guide for 2001.

Clientele come from far and wide to taste the fine wines and sample the exclusive food which is available every lunch time 12.15–2.30 and evenings Tuesday–Saturday 7–9. Lunchtime meals range from pan fried Mediterranean king prawns cooked in smoked garlic butter and white wine to sizzling chicken fajitas served with homemade salsa, guacamole, soured cream and floured tortillas. Also a range of snacks like ploughman's and interesting sandwiches. Dinner appetisers include a smoked chicken Caesar salad and carpaccio of beef followed by roast fresh halibut, Spanish paella, breast of Barbery duck, fresh loin of tuna salad, fresh penne pasta and a traditional Greek salad.

Opening times 11.30–2.30 and 5.30–11. Summer all day at weekends, winter all day on Sunday.

Telephone: 01342 822363.

Pub is situated just south from the B2110 2 miles east of Forest Row.

Approx. distance of walk: 4¼ miles O.S.Map No 188 TQ 452/335.

Park in the lane at the front.

A very peaceful and enjoyable walk along country lanes, across farm land and through Possingford Wood crossing Pooh Sticks Bridge. Apart from the occasional muddy patch the going is good underfoot.

1. Leave the pub and turn left walking up the lane to the junction then turn right into Holyhill on the road signed to Hartford. Cross the main road to join the signed footpath opposite and follow the narrow path down and into the adjoining field. Bearing right walk over to the stile in the far hedge, through the trees and into the field. Make your way across the centre towards the distant house then pass through the gap into the field ahead and keep walking beside the hedge until you reach the stile. Go out into the lane and turn right.

2. Follow the lane for just under a mile before reaching the road then carefully cross over into the drive opposite. Keep straight ahead at the first fork bearing right at the second to pick up the footpath just beyond the farm entrance. An attractive gully, shaded by an overhead canopy of trees, soon leads you to Pooh Sticks Bridge immortalized by A.A.Milne. Cross to the far bank and keep walking through the trees until you reach the lane then turn right.

3. In half a mile bear right over the river and a short distance further on go up the steps on the left and through the gate to pick up the footpath leading into the field. Keeping close to the hedge on the left walk straight across to the stile on the far side and maintain direction, through the gateway leaving the field by the kissing gate, turning right into the lane, carefully walking the short distance uphill to the pub.

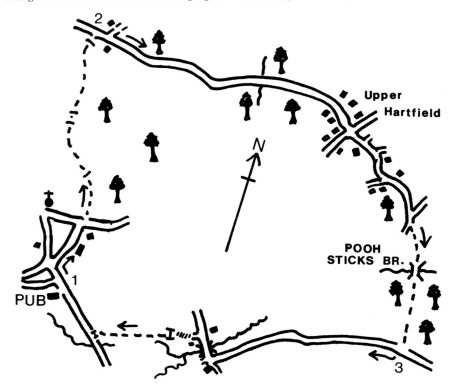

Pooh Sticks Bridge

Bluebell Woods at Cowbeech

Merrie Harriers, Cowbeech

The atmospheric main bar of this old coaching inn has a beamed ceiling, part panelled and part painted walls and a massive curved high back settle beside the inglenook fireplace. Trophies on the wall, old horse brasses and a book case help create that cosy parlour feel. There is an attractive beamed dining area at the opposite end extending into "The Old Stables". The area is fully carpeted with comfortable country style furnishings and heated by an open fire from a small brick fireplace. At the back is a lovely summer conservatory with light wood dining tables and chairs, a terrace and more tables in the pretty back garden.

The inn is a freehouse well run by the new owners who took over in August 2000. Regular real ale includes Harvey's Sussex Best plus a guest together with a fine wine list and single malt whiskies.

Food is available every day during each opening session. Blackboard specials such as a half rack of lamb with red currant and salmon fillet with fresh mint and watercress sauce supplement the printed menus. Lunchtime snacks range from sandwiches and ploughman's to fresh sauté garlic mushrooms and deep-fried Brie wrapped in almonds. Main courses include the house speciality 'Sussex smokie'–fresh haddock topped with butterfly prawns and a homemade cheese sauce, traditional sausage and mash, home-cooked ham, egg and chips and steak and ale pie also vegetarian meals like homemade wild mushroom, leek and Stilton bake and baked broccoli and cauliflower cheese. Additional evening meals include 'Harriers' mixed grill and grilled breast of duck.

Weekday opening times 12–2.30 and 6.15–11, Saturday 11.30–2.30 and 6–11, Sunday 12–2.30 and 7–10.30.

Families welcome, dogs in the garden and the bar only.

Telephone: 01323 833108.

Walk No. 11

Village signposted from the A27 at Herstmonceux.

Approx. distance of walk: 4½ miles. O.S.Map No 199 TQ 618/146.

Park at the front, the side of the pub or in the lane opposite.

An enjoyable walk across farm land, through bluebell woods and along peaceful country lanes. Whilst not over demanding the wooded areas can be very muddy after heavy rain.

1. Leave the pub turning right and in one hundred paces turn right again into the lane signed to Warbleton. Just before reaching the first house on the right there is a farm gate leading into the field on the left. Whilst this is the official 'Right of way' it has not been maintained and is now impassable so until something happens you must continue along the lane until you reach the bend and the next farm gate on the left.

2. Turn left here onto the concrete drive, pass through a second gate and head up to the farm house. Go through the gate and follow the track round and beyond up the tarred drive which gradually rises, past cottages, to join the lane. Immediately on you left are steps leading to a stile. Climb up into the field and bear left making for the gate in the far boundary. Enter the bluebell wood following the path through to the gate on the far side and into the field. Bearing slightly right walk up the rise to the stile, cross into the field and head up to the top keeping close to the field boundary on the right.

3. Go out into the lane and turn right and in three hundred paces look for a short track on the left leading to a stile. Bearing half right walk over to the stile in the fence and maintain direction over a couple more stiles then through the gate and across to one last stile, out onto the track turning left into the lane.

4. In a very short distance turn left into the entrance to Greenway Fruit Farm, signed Studdings Lane. Go through the gate on the left of the barn and follow the main track through the orchard bearing left when you reach the field entrance. Walk down, and round, beside the hedge soon to reach the metal gate allowing access to the attractive woodland path. Cross both bridges and turn left up the wide track to meet the lane. Take the next turning left at the minor cross roads then left again when you reach the lane back down to the pub.

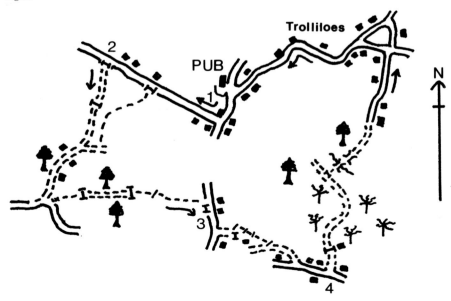

The Bull, Ditchling

The colourful summer display of window boxes and hanging baskets set against the neat white exterior of The Bull is a pretty sight in the High Street of Ditchling. Inside the heavily beamed main bar of this lovely period pub is dominated by a massive brick inglenook fireplace housing a warm log fire in a raised grate. Assorted furnishings consist of high and low back wooden settles, sturdy wooden tables and chairs and a large central refectory table on a wooden floor. There is a very similar carpeted dining room and an attractive rear garden seating up to one hundred people. No music.

The inn is a freehouse currently offering Harvey's Best, Gales HSB and Flowers Original. There is a 20 bin international wine list.

Food is available during the week 12–2.30 and 6–9.30, Saturday and Sunday all day 12–9.30. The printed menu lists a selection of snacks including ploughman's and sandwiches etc. and starters like a salad of Stilton and shallots finished with apples and caramelised in brandy and a duo of smoked salmon and gravadlax with a lemon and olive oil dressing, salad and granary bread. Heading the main courses are Sussex smokie—a gratin of smoked trout, leeks and tomato in a cheese sauce, spicy crab cakes, root vegetable crumble, lamb kofta plus traditional meals like steak and kidney and Guinness pie and good old bangers and mash. A roast is served on Sunday.

Children welcome also dogs on a lead in the pub and garden.

Weekday opening times all day 11–11, Sunday 12–10.30.

Overnight accommodation in 4 en-suite rooms.

Telephone: 01273 843147. Fax: 857787.

Walk No. 12

Village lies at the junction of the B2112 and B2116 south from Burgess Hill.

Approx. distance of walk: 3½ miles O.S. Map No. 198 TQ 326/153.

Although the pub has its own large car park you can park anywhere in the road at the front.

A fairly demanding but very enjoyable, scenic walk up onto the Ditchling Beacon the highest point on the South Downs.

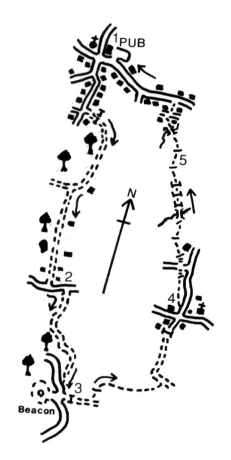

1. Turn left from the pub downhill into South Street soon to turn left into Beacon Road, it is signed, to Ditchling Beacon 1¾. Keep walking until you reach a signed bridleway on the left. Follow the track though the two wooden gates, round to the right and across the driveway to the house. Keep straight ahead passed the vineyard, up to the lane and turn left.

2. In fifty paces turn right onto the bridleway signed, to The Beacon. The fairly demanding track climbs steadily though the nature reserve eventually joining the road near the top. Having reached the gate on the left but before descending it is worth going into the car park on the right to enjoy the view from the beacon. At 814 feet high it is the highest point on this part of the Downs.

3. Pass through the gate beside the dew pond and make your way across the grass to the stile in the fence on the left, go over and bear right following the well trodden path down the hillside taking care as there is a steep drop on the left. Upon reaching the finger post bear left, pass through the wooden gate and follow the path through the trees down to the gate at the bottom of the track, through the farm and up to the road.

4. Walk straight across onto the Ditchling road keeping to the grass verge on the left soon to merge with the signed footpath. Further ahead cross the drive climbing the steps opposite to the stile and enter the field. Maintain your direction negotiating a couple more stiles and the plank bridge then enter and leave the deer enclosures through the high kissing gates.

5. Bear right into the field making for the stile in the hedge then follow the path across to a squeeze stile and turn right through a second and onto the path between the houses. Enter the road, turn right and immediately left onto the signed path between the houses. Go through the kissing gate, up to the road and turn left walking about half a mile back to the pub.

Ditchling Beacon

The Seven Sisters

The Tiger Inn, East Dean

Few pubs can boast a more attractive setting than the delightful Tiger Inn. Flanked by the Downs the pub occupies a sunny position on the cottage-lined green. This long, low white painted, tiled pub has pretty window boxes and roses climbing the walls with flower tubs and picnic benches on the front terrace. Inside there are two attractive rooms the smaller 'Parlour Bar' has simple furnishings which include a large curved wooden settle, whilst the 'Kitchen Bar' has a heavily beamed ceiling and more wooden settles on the bare stone floor. Various horse brasses and other interesting regalia decorate the large stone fireplace and dark walls.

The well stocked bar boasts some interesting wines such as Ch. La Tour-saint-Bonnet and Ch. Pontesac and three real ales, Harveys Best Bitter, Adnams Broadside and Batemans XB.

Bar food, is available every lunchtime 12–2 and in evenings 6.30–9. Listed daily on the blackboard are the usual pub favourites such as assorted ploughman's and jumbo sausages plus Breton fish soup. Tiger regulars include steak and kidney pie and fried fresh fish and chips. In addition there are specials which in the summer consists mainly of fresh fish and shellfish such as crabs and prawns. There could also be chicken and vegetable pie and fusilli tombego which is pasta twists with a tasty tomato sauce, salad and garlic bread also beef bourguignon and a vegetable casserole with goat's cheese. Sweets range from Fanny's French apple tart to Fifi's French lemon tart.

Children are not permitted in either bar if under 14; dogs are welcome on a lead.

Weekday opening times 11–3 and 6–11. Open all day Saturday and Sunday. Telephone: 01323 423209.

Village signed from the A259 west off Eastbourne. The turning opposite the service station leads straight down to the free car park.

Approx. distance of walk: 3¼ miles. O.S.Map No.199 TV 557/976.

Although you can park in the village it is best to use the free car park.

A most enjoyable scenic walk on National Trust land through Crowlink, along the Seven Sisters cliffs and back across Went Hill. Although steep in some places the going is easy and good underfoot. The Seven Sisters Sheep Centre, open daily from mid march to early September, is a family-run farm where children can help with daily bottle feeding sessions.

1. Leave the pub turning right, walk up to the lane and turn left. Turn right at the bend and pass through the gate onto the signed footpath. Bearing left walk up the grassy combe and just beyond the edge of the woods climb the rise making your way across to the gate in the top right-hand corner. Go through into the field turning right towards the gate, out to the track and turn left.

2. Pass through the gate beside the cattle grid onto the tarred bridleway. Crowlink and Birling Gap are owned by The National Trust and visitors may wander where they wish. Enter the field beyond the dwellings and continue ahead through a second gate, down past the finger post towards the cliffs then follow the path up to the left keeping well away from the edge. The path affords some spectacular views of The Seven Sisters a series of chalk spurs with dry valleys between.

3. Continue ahead past the monument then climb the high stile walking to the top of the rise. Keep on past the obelisk, up the next cliff after which take the well trodden path inland beside the fence passing through the gate on the left signed, to East Dean 1 mile. Keep to the path up the hillside heading towards the red roofed building go past and follow the path ahead down through the woods to the gate and into Went Way back to the village and the pub.

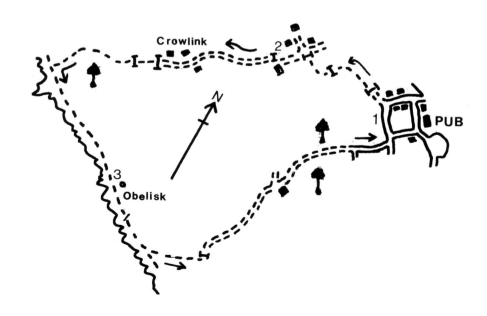

The Ram Inn, Firle

My ideal pub must be unpretentious, simply furnished but comfortable and ideally heated by an open fire in winter. I look for a friendly, dedicated landlord who can serve me a pint of well conditioned real ale and extremely good pub food. A tall order you might say but such pubs do exist. Sitting beneath the South Downs is the lovely village of Firle–the countryseat of the Gage family, responsible for the introduction of the greengage and at its centre is The Ram Inn, which is just such a pub. The main bar of The Ram has solid tables and chairs on a bare wooden floor, part panelled walls and an open fire. There is a similar cosy 'snug' where smoking is not permitted and more room in the old courthouse upstairs which is used as a family room in the winter with many children's games and colouring books. Outside there is play equipment plus a separate quiet area for adults without children. Live folk music 2nd Monday and 1st Wednesday.

The inn is a family friendly freehouse very enthusiastically run by the amiable long standing licensee Michael Wooller in partnership with his son, Keith, partner Nikki Bullen and his family. Drinks include ten wines by the glass, Addlestones cider plus real ales, Harvey's Best Bitter, Cuckoo Bitter and Shepherd Neame and Goldings Bitter.

Excellent bar food served all day 12–9 with cream teas between 3 & 5.30 includes soup, baguettes, filled jackets and interesting ploughman's. A good homemade range of vegetarian meals is listed daily on the specials board and there is a separate children's menu with toddler options even baby food is on sale and there is a microwave for customer's use. In addition to daily specials there is a choice of fish, pasta and meat dishes such as a Cumberland ring sausage with mash and mushy peas and rack of pork loin ribs. A good sweet list includes local Willett's ice cream and some good old favourites such as apple crumble. Sunday roast.

Weekday opening 11.30–11, Sunday 12–10.30.
Telephone: 01273 858222.

Village is signed south from the A27 about 4 mile east of Lewes.

Approx. distance of walk: $1\frac{3}{4}$ miles. O.S.Map No.198 TQ 469/074.

Park outside the pub, in the lane opposite or as suggested by the Firle Estate in the free car park signed a short distance along the lane leading from the main road.

A short nut nevertheless enjoyable and interesting ramble through this pretty little village and into Firle Park. Home to the Gage family since the 15th century the house is open to the public from May to the end of September on bank holidays, Sundays, Wednesdays and Thursdays from 2 p.m. till 5 p.m. Good underfoot and the absence of stiles makes it an ideal family walk perfect for a summers evening.

1. From the pub take the lane opposite through the village forking right at the post office. Walk past the church and keep straight ahead onto the bridleway following the track round to the left beside the wall.
2. After just over a quarter of a mile take the signed bridleway on the left. Upon reaching the pair of cottages go through the gate on the left set back behind the small car parking area.

3. Keeping a fairly straight line make your way across the park where you can enjoy a splendid view of Firle Place. Cross the drive by the fingerpost, signed to the village, and keep walking until you reach the kissing gate. Pass through onto the track, walk up to the village and turn right back to the pub.

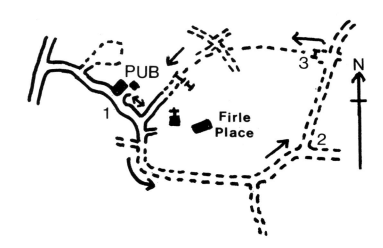

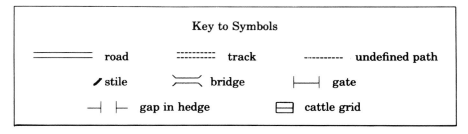

Key to Symbols

═══════ road	---------- track	---------- undefined path
✒ stile	⟩══⟨ bridge	⊢——⊣ gate
⊣ ⊢ gap in hedge	⊟ cattle grid	

37

The Griffin Inn, Fletching

This delightful inn dates back from the 16th-century and last changed hands in 1978. Totally in keeping with this ancient village the cosy oak panelled and beamed seating area of the bar is warmed by a roaring winter log fire behind which is the cosy, bare boarded servery. There is a separate restaurant and children's room, a separate public bar and picnic tables in the landscaped rear garden. Occasional theme nights are a feature of the inn, which are listed in their own news-letter.

Owned by Bridget and Nigel Pullan this popular freehouse is well run by the landlord David Pullan. The well stocked bar includes a constantly changing list of real ales which might include Horsam Best, Harvey's Armada and Sussex Bitter plus guests such as the delightful pale Tanglefoot from Hall & Woodhouse and Ruddles Best Bitter.

Excellent food, served seven days a week 12–2.30 and 7–9.30, is predominately seasonal drawing customers from a very wide area. On my last visit the tempting blackboard menu listed celeriac and cider soup, brochette of kidneys and bacon and warm salad of pigeon breast followed by Lancashire lamb pie, and good old favourite sausage and mash with onion gravy. Also sole and scallops, Sussex smokies and baked halibut with a Provencale sauce. Restaurant meals might include Mediterranean chicken salad with olives, capers, roasted peppers and courgettes or pan fried John Dory with ginger and chive sauce. There are, of course, snacks like ploughman's plus enormous (off the plate) sausages made by the butcher opposite. Weather permitting there are summer barbecues.

Accommodation is available in seven four-poster beds plus one twin bedded room.

Children are always welcome and there is no objection to well behaved dogs.

Weekday opening times 12–2.30ish and 6–11. All day at weekends.

Telephone: 01825 722890.

The village lies to the east of Haywards Heath and can be reached from the A272 or the A275.

Approx. distance of walk: $2\frac{3}{4}$ miles. O.S.Map No 198 TQ 428/235.

The pub has its own car park but you can park quite safely in the road outside.

A very enjoyable walk easy going for the most part across farmland and on peaceful country lanes. Nearby the 100-acre landscaped gardens of Sheffield Park are open to the public from April to November, Tuesday to Saturday from 11 a.m. till 6 p.m.

1. Cross the road from the pub turning right and then follow the little path through the churchyard bearing left across to the kissing gate in the back hedge. Go into the field and bear left making your way to the gate in the far corner beyond the trig point. Pass into the field and continue in the same direction towards the stile in the hedge. Go over onto the grass path and bear right across to the stile beside the gate, enter the field and bear half right to the stile in the far hedge.

2. After passing through a narrow strip of very attractive woodland abundant with wild flowers the path leads up to a stile and into a field. Bear right in the direction of the waymark to the stile in the hedge and then head towards the distant house. After passing through the gap in the hedge bear right across to the wooden bridge, over the stream into the field, through the small gate beyond the barn, up the drive to the lane and turn right.

3. It is very peaceful and attractive with many wild flowers in the hedgerows. Turn right at the T junction and in $\frac{3}{4}$ of a mile turn right into the drive of Mallingdown Farm then almost immediately left onto the grass path walking until you reach the tarred dive. Turn right through the farm gate and keep straight ahead past the dwellings, leaving by the farm gate at the back and through a second gate into the field beyond. Walk down to the stile beside the gate and join the wide grass track leading into the field.

4. After following the hedge down to the stile, go over and continue in the same direction crossing the stile on the right into the field keeping straight ahead to the footbridge opposite. Cross the stream and make for the stile in the far field then bear slightly left climbing until you reach the stile in the hedge leading out onto the track. Turn right and right again when you reach the metal farm gates then go through the gate into the field on the left. Keep straight ahead past the farm building to the church retracing your steps back to the pub.

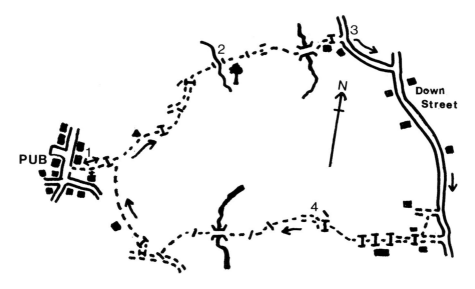

The Half Moon, Friar's Gate

Close to Ashdown Forest this excellent family pub has a relaxed and friendly atmosphere. The comfortable bare boarded and carpeted L shaped bar has a nice ambience for both drinkers and diners alike further enhanced by the warm winter log fire. Several interesting artefacts are on display. There is seating in the front garden and more in the large rear garden where there is also an extensive children's play area which includes bouncy castle, climbing frame, swings, 5-side-football pitch, and a French boules pitch.

The inn is a freehouse well run by new licensees Peter Cutbush and Celia Bottomley offering a choice of Harvey's real ales and other drinks.

Pub food is available Monday–Friday 12–2, weekends (2.30) and evenings Wednesday–Saturday 7–9 but not Sunday evening. Snacks listed on the menu include jacket potatoes with a choice of fillings, sandwiches, baguettes, beef burgers and ploughman's. Followed by home-carved ham, eggs and fries and served with salad, Mexican beef chilli, Speldhurst sausages, eggs and fries, traditional steak and kidney pudding, breaded scampi and omelettes made to order with various fillings. Specials are listed daily on the blackboard and could include authentic Indian curries, gammon steak, battered cod and a Spanish omelette. There is a roast lunch on Sunday plus five choices for children.

Dogs and children are both equally welcome.

No overnight accommodation but a small tent by permission.

Opening times 12–3 and 6–11, all day Saturday and Sunday.

Telephone: 01892 661270.

The pub is situated on the B2188 at Friar's Gate north west from Crowborough. The entrance to the pub is from the lane at the side.

Approx: distance of walk: $4\frac{1}{4}$ miles. O.S.Map No.188 TQ 498/335

Park in the lane at the side or in the pub's own large car park by the stream.

Easy underfoot this very enjoyable walk at first takes you into Five Hundred Acre Wood and then along a wide track to Withyham with its ancient church. After entering Buckhurst Park, but before reaching the pub there are two attractive woodland paths to follow, a cross field path and a peaceful country lane.

1. Leave the pub turning right into the road and continue walking up hill until you reach the wide forestry track on the right. Follow it through the woods for about half a mile then take the right fork leading to the house. Almost immediately turn right onto the narrow footpath skirting the field before rejoining the track through the gate.

2. Simply follow the track past the church of St Michael & All Angels to eventually reach the main road at Withyham then turn right. The first mention of a church on the site was as early as 1291 the present church was re-built in 1672 after a lightning strike almost completely destroyed the original building.

3. Upon reaching the Dorset Arms, a good halfway refreshment stop, go up the drive on the right into Buckhurst Park. Keep walking and upon reaching the lake bear right up the hill and take the signed path on the left up into the woods.

4. Proceed along this attractive path until you reach footpath No 43 signed through a gate in the hedge on the right. Bearing half left walk up the field, over the brow and down the far side making for the stile in the left-hand hedge beyond the dwellings. Climb over onto the wooded path and turn right walking down to the road at the bottom. Cross over into the lane opposite then bear right at the fork back to the pub.

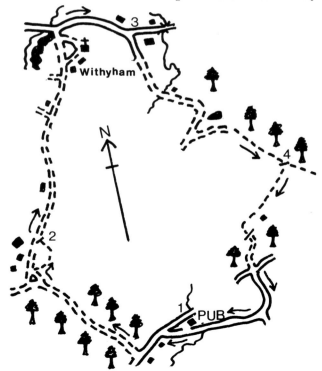

The Gun Inn, Gun Hill

Presumably having derived its name from the local quarries, which once produced iron for guns this lovely pub, enjoying a quiet country setting, dates back to the 18th century when it was just a farmhouse selling beer. Later it was owned by Kemptown Ales, a photograph taken at the time showing the small weather-boarded pub can be seen hanging in the bar. The original kitchen with its Aga, still used today, is now incorporated into the heavily beamed main bar, both areas having retained their ancient red brick floors. Two comfortable dining areas on the far side of the central fireplace are comfortably furnished with farmhouse tables and chairs and decorated with old pictures and brightly shining copper and brass. In one there is an open fireplace close to the servery. Outside there is a large beer garden with a safe children's play area.

The inn is a freehouse beautifully kept and lovingly cared for with glorious summer flower displays. Two well-kept real ales dispensed by handpump are Harvey's Best and Adnams Bitter.

The result of good healthy food all freshly prepared on the premises led to the pub receiving the 'Heartbeat Award' for healthy eating options. All items kind to your heart are marked accordingly even Flora can be selected as an option to butter. Served seven days a week 12–2.15 (Sunday 2) and 6–9.15 daily specials such as homemade turkey, ham and leek pie and lamb hotpot go along side meals like salmon and spinach en croute and grandma's chicken casserole. The main menu offers French bread snacks, homemade soup, salads and various grills. Fresh fish specials might include Sussex smokies, fresh salmon and plaice brought up from Newhaven and there is a very good vegetarian selection. The more comprehensive evening selection features a seafood platter and fillet steak Wellington. Children have their own menu.

Children and dogs both equally welcome.

Weekday opening times 11.30–3 and 6–11 Sunday 12–3 and 6–10.30.

Telephone: 01285 872361.

Village signed west from the A267 between Hailsham and Heathfield.

Approx. distance of walk: 3 miles O.S.Map No. 199 TQ 567/146.

Park on the front forecourt or in the gravel park at the side.

A very enjoyable walk across farmland, through bluebell woods and on peaceful country lanes. It is easy going for the most part except for the path through the woods from Stream Mill. Be warned though in can be extremely muddy in places after wet weather.

1. Start from the stile in the hedge behind the children's play area walking straight across the field to meet the hedge then continue to the stile, go out into the lane and turn left. In just over half a mile, after reaching a group of dwellings and where the lane starts to rise, there is a bungalow on the left set well back from the lane named Toteridge.

2. Pass through the entrance gates and immediately turn left walking around the pond and lawn keeping to the path beside the trees. Part way round you will reach some steps cut into the bank on the left. Go down into the bluebell wood, cross the plank bridge following the path through the woods to the stile. Keep to the signed path and after entering a clearing make your way across to the stile on the far side. Head up the field to the farm gate, turn left, pass through a similar gate and bear half right up the field to the gate in the top hedge. Keep straight ahead over a couple more stiles, go out into the lane and turn right.

3. In fifty paces cross the road and climb the steps to the stile. Keeping close to the boundary walk down and round the field to the plank bridge and stiles at the bottom, cross over onto the grass path and head up through the orchard to the gate at the top, go out into the lane turning left.

4. Almost immediately take the signed public bridleway on the right. The track drops steadily through woods before reaching Stream Mill. On the left is a stile leading into a field. The footpath runs beside the fence up to the stile at the top. Cross over into the woods and follow the path ahead eventually entering a clearing. Bearing slightly to the left make your way over to the gap in the far hedge, pass through and turn right walking round the field and out into the lane.

5. Walk straight across through the gate opposite, through a second gate and onto the signed bridleway. Looking over your left shoulder is a delightful timber framed dwelling. Bear right, pass through the metal gate into Friths Farm and on to the concrete road back to the pub.

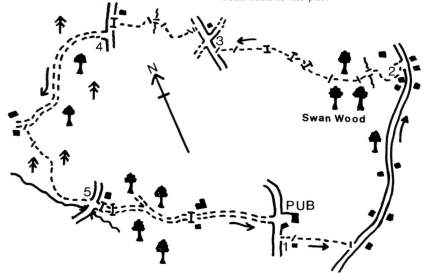

Anchor Inn, Hartfield

The Anchor Inn was built during the reign of Edward IV in 1465 and at that time was a thatched farm dwelling. The property first became a registered ale house in 1745 and a list of all the owners since that date is displayed in the comfortably furnished beamed bar. Several old village photographs hang on the wall above the wood burning stove, a grandfather clock stands close by and there is a framed collection of old cigarette cards. A door at the back leads through to a small games room and across the corridor is an attractive dining room.

The inn is a freehouse offering at least six real ales in the winter and up to twelve in the summer. Typically there might be Wadworth 6X, Harvey's Sussex Bitter, Marston's Pedigree and Flowers Original.

A very good choice of food cooked by the proprietor is available seven days a week. Daily specials such as French onion soup and moules mariniere supplement the bar menu which besides the usual snacks of ploughman's and sandwiches offers tasty starters of barbecued pork spare ribs, hot garlic prawns cooked in their shells, Camembert fritters with Cumberland sauce and spicy potato skins. There are several fish dishes which might include smoked haddock au gratin and prawns and a prawn and crab curry. Also listed are lamb kidneys Creole and London pie. On one visit the blackboard menu listed chicken and pork pate, half a dozen snails, gratin of crab, sole, scampi cingalai, grilled scallops with bacon, veal escalope with Stilton, lamb noisettes and chateaubriand for two. Vegetarians have a good choice of dishes which could range from macaroni with leeks and tarragon to cheese and spinach pancakes. Children have their own menu.

Families are welcome and dogs too on a lead.

Opening times all day 11–11, Sunday 12–10.30.

Telephone: 01892 770424.

Pub situated on the B2026 in the centre of the village close to the church.

Approx. distance of walk: $3\frac{1}{2}$ miles. O.S. Map No 188 TQ 478/357.

Park at the pub, in the lane outside or the main village street.

An ideal walk for all the family on well established paths, across farm land, through woods and along the attractive course of the old railway line.

1. Leave the pub turning right and right again through the village walking down as far as the bend. Keep straight ahead on the B2026 and just before the bridge take the tarred path on the right, signposted, into the Forest Way Country Park. Turn left under the bridge and just before reaching the next bridge climb the bank on the right, pass through the gate into the field waking round beside the hedge to the double gates. Cross the bridge and keep walking on the wide track up through the trees until you reach a cross track, pass behind the barn to re-join the track eventually reaching the farm lane and turn left.

2. Walk into St Ives Farm and upon reaching the stile on the left, opposite the dwelling, cross into the field and turn right, turning left when you reach the finger post. Bear right across the field making for the hedge gap in the far right-hand corner. Cross the stream and the strip of land, pass through the hedge bearing left down the field to the finger post. Keep straight ahead through the copse soon to bear right over the bridge, climb the bank to the path and turn left.

3. Upon reaching the old railway line turn left and walk for a mile at which point you will see a stile on the right. Go into the field keeping straight ahead to pick up the path which leads into the playing fields and back to the road opposite the pub.

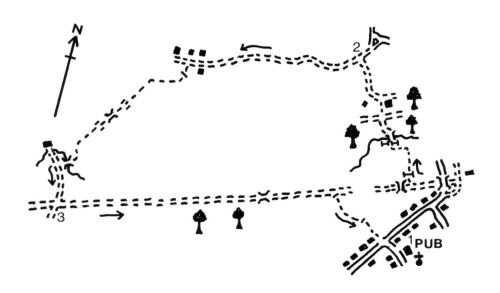

The Stag, Hastings

Hastings is well served with pubs there being no less than 17 in the town alone. A particularly good one is the 16th century Stag named by CAMRA in 1993 as 'Sussex Pub of the Year'. Situated on the high pavement in All Saints Street the lovely, ancient, bare-boarded main bar has a heavily timbered ceiling and two open log fireplaces. During work on the larger chimney the mummified bodies of two cats were found which are now displayed in a case on the wall. The story tells that they were once the cats of a witch named Hannah Clarke. During the great plague of 1665–1666 it was commonly believed that cats and dogs were to blame and so it came that Hannah's cats were bricked into the fireplace.

The pub is owned by Shepherd & Neame. Four of their well-conditioned real ales served by hand pump include Best Bitter, Bishop's Finger, Master Brew and Spitfire.

Good freshly cooked bar food, available at lunch times from Tuesday to Saturday, includes soup, deep fired crispy mushrooms and 'Stag' mixed dip – scampi, crispy mushrooms and baby sweet corn with mayonnaise followed by homemade Hastings fish pie, individual homemade steak and kidney, half a rack of barbecue pork ribs, Scotch rump steak and a mixed grill. For vegetarians there is ploughman's, well dressed potatoes and French bread sandwiches. A separate menu is available for children

Opening times, Monday to Friday are from 12–3 and 6–11

Families are welcome and there is no objection to well behaved dogs on a lead. One room is set aside for overnight accommodation.

Telephone: 01424 425734

The pub is situated in the Old Town on the high pavement in All Saints Street which leads straight down to the seafront.

Approx. distance of walk: 4 miles O.S Map No.199 TQ 828/098.

Parking can be a problem close to the pub although limited parking is permitted in the road. Alternatively use the pay car park on the sea front or if you are lucky use one of the free spaces in the road.

A sometimes bracing but extremely enjoyable, scenic walk in the Hastings Country Park along the cliff top path to Fairlight Glen, returning beside the reservoir through Ecclesbourne Glen. To help you find your way there are a series of conveniently situated bollards. Although a little strenuous at times the going is mostly good underfoot making it an ideal walk for all the family.

1. Leave the pub and turn left taking time to admire some of the ancient buildings shortly to turn left into Crown Lane. Walk to the top, climb the steps opposite and when you reach the lift continue ahead up into Hastings Country Park, past the beacon keeping fairly close to the fence on the right.
2. Fork right at the finger post, down the steps into Ecclesbourne Glen then turn right at the next path junction into the valley and climb the steep steps on the far side. Whilst fairly demanding seats have been provided at suitable intervals. Continue left following the yellow waymark signs until you reach bollard 7.
3. Follow the sign to Fairlight Glen ¼ mile. After descending a fairly long and steep flight of steps and reaching bollard 8 take the path on the left, signed to Fairlight Glen Upper. A very colourful display of wild flowers and interesting grasses carpet the ground including bluebells, pink campion, blue ground ivy and yellow archangel to name but a few. At bollard 9 take the path

on the left, signed to Barley Lane, following it up and round, through the gate and out onto the track at the top turning left.
4. Keep walking and after the second gate take the track on the left opposite the footpath to Ore. Further ahead cross the stile on the right and walk down into the trees then fork right at bollard 6 and further on branch right again on the path beside the reservoir; occasionally glimpsed through the trees.
5. At bollard 5 fork right steadily climbing to a path near the top then bear left onto the hillside path where you have a lovely view of the bay. Eventually the path reaches the bollard passed earlier in the walk at this point turn right up the bank towards the sports pavilion, pass through the picnic area and head across the putting green turning left at the fingerpost on the far side.
6. Turn left at the next finger post and join the path on the right gently descending behind the church into the lane. Turn left and then right at the next passage back down to the pub.

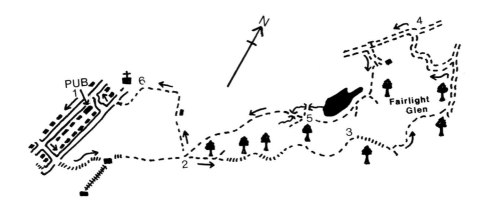

The lift to the Hastings Country Park

Fairlight Glen

The Queens Head Inn, Icklesham

Originally dwellings and a butchers shop dating from 1632 this lovely pub first became an ale house in 1831, the distinctive white painted and tile hung façade hiding the timeworn interior. All on different levels the main areas are divided by ancient wooden screening and exposed beams which support the high pitched roof. In one area there is a warm wood burning stove whilst another has a roaring log fire in a large inglenook fireplace. A separate area is set aside for non-smokers but the best seats in summer are without doubt in the garden where one can sit and admire one of the best views in East Sussex overlooking the Brede Level. There is a boules pitch and music on Tuesdays.

The pub is a freehouse very well run by the owners since 1984. A mecca for real ale lovers the constantly changing list can include up to six at any one time ranging from Cotleigh Tawny Bitter, Pett Progress from Forge Brewery, Old Speckled Hen and Hop Back's Crop Circle to winter ales, Harvey's Old and Ringwood's Old Thumper. CAMRA Sussex Pub of the Year 1998. Biddenden cider and wines on list.

Excellent food is available weekdays 12–2.45 and 6.15–9.45, weekends all day 12–9.45. From the bar menu snacks include soft herring roes on toast, prawn fritters, garlic mayonnaise, half a pint of prawns and home-cooked ham and eggs with French fries. There is a good choice of salads, ploughman's and sandwiches plus homemade dishes like chicken, ham and mushroom pie, Stilton and apricot macaroni cheese, broccoli and cauliflower cheese and leek Brie and bacon pasta.

Various steaks and grills are in addition to fresh fish daily specials and home-made soups.

Children welcome, dogs on leads inside and out.

Open all day 11–11, Sunday 12–10.30.

Telephone: 01424 814552.

Walk No. 20

Village on the A259 between Hasting and Rye. Take the lane north opposite the church the inn is on the right at the end of a short track.

Approx. distance of walk: 4¼ miles O.S. Maps 199 TQ 878/166.

There is ample parking at the pub plus more space in the lane.

A fairly long but very enjoyable scenic walk across farm land and through the Brede Level following the River Brede for much of the walk. Not too demanding it is mostly good underfoot.

1. From the pub turn right into the lane, walk to the end and keep straight ahead on to the footpath walking until you reach a signed path on the right. Go over into the field keeping straight ahead down to the plank bridge at the bottom. Cross into the field and maintain direction close to the boundary, pass through the gate and continue beside the hedge towards the gate.

2. Head up the farm road, past the dwellings, walking as far as the drive on the right, signed to Snaylham House. Turn into the drive, walk past the house and farm buildings turning right when you reach the gravel track.

3. After walking for some distance the track passes over the railway line then heads across the Brede Level before reaching the River Brede. Ignore the bridge but turn right, cross the stile into the field then simply follow the path beside the river for about a mile and a half negotiating the occasional stile and gate.

4. Eventually when you reach the bridge leading to Float Farm turn right, cross the field to the railway crossing then go over the stile into the field keeping straight ahead beside the brook. After several stiles cross the cattle bridge and bear half right up the hill to the stile beside the farm gate in the top fence. Climb into the field and proceed towards the stile beyond allowing direct access to the car park of the pub.

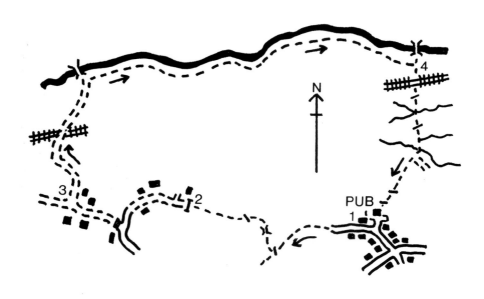

The Bell Inn, Iden

The small village of Iden lies close to the border with Kent and a mile or so from The Royal Military Canal cut in 1806. Dating from around the eighteenth century the attractive white boarded and tile hung exterior of the Bell is bedecked in summer with a colourful display of hanging baskets. Inside there are two main areas one has a games table and dartboard the other a low, heavily beamed wooden ceiling and partioned dining area to the side. It is comfortably furnished with an attractive fireplace in the end wall. Assorted furnishings consist of some comfortable, wooden wall settles whilst dried flowers and hops add to the attractive decorations. Outside there is large lawned beer garden with picnic benches, a children's play area and a petanque pitch.

The inn is a freehouse but was about to change hands at the time of this update. Three real ales presently on offer include Green King IPA, Abbot Ale and Sussex Bitter.

All meals, freshly prepared to order, are served all week between 12 and 2 and 7–9. From the menu there is a choice of pizzas freshly made to order with your own choice of topping plus the usual bar snacks of ploughman's and sandwiches. Smoked salmon pate could be followed by grilled steaks, chicken cordon bleu, traditional gammon steak, lasagne and chicken tikka. Vegetarians might want to choose cauliflower cheese or spinach and mushroom lasagne whilst fresh fish lovers can order one of the daily specials. Booking only though for the three course Sunday lunch.

Weekday opening times are from 11–3 and 6–11.

Children are welcome in the dining area and dogs in the bar or garden on a lead.

Telephone: 01797 280242

Walk No. 21

Village located north of Rye on the B2082.

Approx. distance of walk: 2¼ miles. O.S.Map No. 189 TQ 917/238.

Park at the side of the pub or in the village.

A short but interesting walk mostly across farm land on field paths, tracks and country lanes. At the time of writing some paths were badly in need of waymarking hopefully it has now been completed.

1. Leave the pub turning right, cross into Grove Lane and immediately take the signed footpath on the left next to the war memorial. Climb the stile into the field leaving by the gate opposite. Follow the footpath to the next gate, go through into the field and walk round to the stile opposite. Enter the field ahead keeping close to the hedge on the left shortly to reach a gap in the hedge. Climb into the adjoining field, cross to the gate on the far side, go out into the lane and turn right.

2. Almost immediately turn right onto the gravel track following it for some distance before reaching a left-hand bend. On the right is a gate leading into an orchard. Take the main path down, between the fruit trees to meet the hedge at the bottom and turn right walking until you find a gap in the hedge on the left. Climb down into the adjoining field and keep straight ahead to the far corner, cross the stream and pass through the green gate on the right keeping to the well worn path up towards the finger post.

3. Follow the hedge boundary round to the stile at the top and keep straight ahead to the gap walking until you reach the far hedge then turn right. Go through the gate onto the farm road, past the buildings turning into the lane back to the village and the pub.

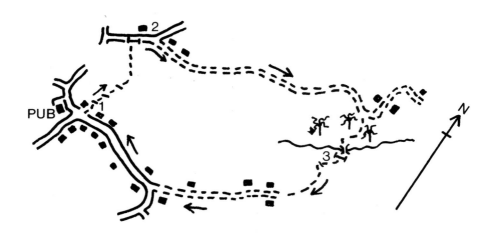

The sketch maps in this book are not necessarily to scale but have been drawn to show the maximum amount of detail.

The Juggs, Kingston

Roses cling to the white painted and tile hung exterior of this delightful 15th century pub set in its own pretty flower filled gardens in a peaceful lane leading to the downs. Warmed by an open log winter fire the lovely cottage bar has a low heavily beamed ceiling, stripped brick or painted walls and decorated throughout with a fascinating display of old curios and well polished copper and brass items. A larger room is reached through a passage way which also doubles as a family room. There is lots of outside seating at the front and at the side together with a large children's play area. The pub is a local for locals as well as encouraging walkers and other passing trade. Background music, functions welcomed.

Until recently a freehouse The Juggs is now owned by Shepherd and Neame the Kent brewers and well run under the supervision of Pete and Sandy Smith. Real ales include Shepherd & Neame's own ales like Spitfire, Masterbrew and seasonal ales, plus Holsten 'Plus' and Oranjeboom lagers also a range of quality wines.

Popular with diners traditional country cooking is available all day, everyday 12–9 (Sunday 8). A printed menu lists the usual bar snacks and supplements the daily changing blackboard, which lists fresh fish dishes and a range of homemade pies. There is a good separate à la carte menu and a traditional Sunday roast.

Children and dogs equally welcome inside and out
Weekday opening all day 11–11 Sunday 12–10.30.
Telephone: 01273 472523. Fax: 01273 483274.

Walk No. 22

Village signed from the roundabout on the A 27 west of Lewes. The inn is located in The Street a short lane leading to the church.

Approx. distance of walk: 2½ miles. O.S.Map No.198 TQ 393/083.

Park in the lane outside or in the pub's own large car park.

A short but very enjoyable, scenic walk which takes you high up on to the downs at Swanborough Hill. Although fairly demanding it is an ideal walk for all the family.

1. From the pub walk back down to the Brighton/Newhaven road and turn right. Keep walking until you reach a footpath on the right signed Swanborough 1 mile. Go up the track and immediately bear left onto the grassy path leading to the stile. Cross into the field and keep straight ahead to the next crossing point then walk beside the farm buildings towards the crossing point on the left.

2. Go over into the yard, out into the lane by the cottages and turn right onto the concrete road. Walk past the cottages following the gravel track as it heads up through the trees. Take the right fork, pass through the gate shortly to enter the field bearing left then keep to the gully up the downs.

3. Before reaching the top turn right and follow the narrow footpath down to the stile, over into the meadow and down to a second stile taking time to enjoy the glorious views. In a few paces go left down the bank following the well trodden path into the trees and up to the stile. Continue along the path finally crossing one last stile onto the track leading to the lane back to the pub.

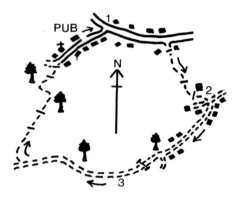

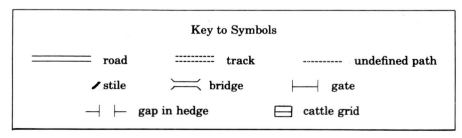

Key to Symbols

road ========   track ----------   undefined path ----------

✔ stile   ⟩—⟨ bridge   ├—┤ gate

⊣ ⊢ gap in hedge   ⊟ cattle grid

The view over Kingston from Swanborough Hill

The White Horse viewed from Litlington

The Plough & Harrow, Litlington

The picturesque village of Litlington lies in a secluded spot in the Cuckmere Valley one of the last remaining unspoilt valleys in Sussex. At its centre is the delightful Plough & Harrow. Although extended over the years the small, original 15th century wattle and daubed pub with its large open fireplace and warm winter log fire still remains but is now reached from the main bar, carpeted, low beamed and tastefully furnished with attractive carved settles and cut down beer barrels. There is an attractive restaurant, candlelit in winter. At the back there is a small beer garden with smart wooden tables and benches. Live music on Friday.

The inn is a freehouse very well run for the last 3 years by the new owners Barry and Ros Richards. From a long and constantly changing list of real ales there are always up to five on offer. On my last visit I had the choice of Hall & Woodhouse Best Bitter and Tanglefoot, also beers from the local Harvey's Brewery.

The pub is popular locally for its good home-cooked food, which can be enjoyed every day of the week 12–2 and 6.30–9. Listed daily on the blackboard there are several starters such as homemade soup, deep fried Camembert and prawns in filo followed by mignons of lamb in a red wine and redcurrant sauce, roast duck with mango coulis and a good selection of fresh fish meals. Vegetarian options might include spinach and roast pepper lasagne. In addition there are the usual pub snacks of ploughman's, filled potatoes and ciabatta rolls. Roast is served on Sunday.

Children are welcome with parents in the restaurant and there is no objection to dogs on a lead in the main bar.

Weekday opening times are from 11.30–3 and 6.30–11.

Telephone: 01323 870632.

Village signed south from the A27 at Wilmington Green 2 miles west of Polegate.

Approx. distance of walk: 3½ miles. O.S.Map No 199 TQ 523/016.

There is car park at the back of the pub also limited space in the road outside.

A very enjoyable and peaceful, scenic walk at first across farm land, through woods and on wide grass tracts leading into Lullington Heath Nature Reserve before returning along a down land bridleway. Although hilly the walk is not too strenuous but can be wet underfoot in the winter.

1. From the pub turn right and further on turn left into the entrance to Clapham Farm. Fork right at the entrance to the house and follow the track, up and round to the right, past the farm buildings into the field beyond keeping to the track beside the hedge on the left. After a good mile pass through the gate and enter the woods keeping to the main path ahead.
2. Upon reaching the fingerpost turn left in the direction of Lullington Heath. Bear left at the next path junction climbing the rise to the gate and enter the nature reserve.

One of the best examples of chalk heath remaining in Britain, the reserve is a colourful patchwork of different types of vegetation. Follow the main track as it rises through the scrub eventually reaching the gate leading out onto the bridleway.
3. Turn left. Keep straight ahead at the first finger post forking left at the second. Looking across to your left you have a good sight of the White Horse carved into the downs. Bear right through the farm, down into the road and turn left back to the pub.

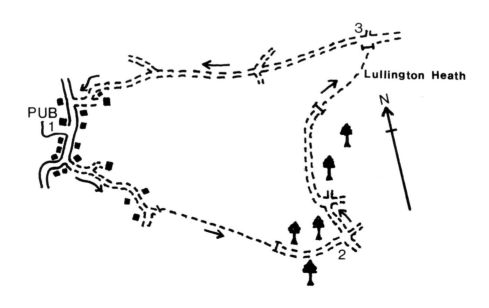

The Rose & Crown Inn, Mayfield

Mayfield is said to be the prettiest village in Sussex certainly many of its ancient, timber studded buildings still line the main high street. The very attractive Rose & Crown, originally a coaching inn, dates from the 16th century. The main bar, divided by a wooden screen, has a low-beamed and boarded ceiling, a warm log fire in the large inglenook fireplace and simple furnishings, which include pew style seats. There is additional seating in a room behind the bar whilst the other, very attractive lower level bar, also has a low-beamed ceiling and is festooned with hop flowers and lots of interesting regalia on the bare brick and painted walls. Candles top the tables in the comfortable restaurant and picnic benches are arranged on the sunny front terrace.

The inn is now owned by Enterprise Inns and run since 2002 by the Perfect Pub Co. The well stocked bar boasts three real ales, Harvey's Best, Adnams Bitter plus a guest ale.

The inn is listed in the many good food guides and justifiably so. Served Monday–Saturday 12–2.30 and 6.30–9.30, Sunday all day 12–9, the bar menu has the usual pub snacks plus dishes like smoked salmon and cream quenelles to baby queen scallops baked in garlic and cheese. Main courses could include homemade pies, beef Wellington, Indonesian chicken with fruit and nuts and mildly spiced in a coconut milk sauce also a half shoulder of Shrewsbury lamb marinated then braised in red wine and fresh herbs. There is a mushroom stroganoff and ratatouille pasta bake for vegetarians, a roast on Sunday and chef's daily specials which might include Corsican chicken breast wrapped in smoked bacon with a sauce of garlic, shallots, olives and sun dried tomatoes or veal, wild boar, gammon and apple pie.

The inn offers excellent overnight accommodation in luxury en-suite rooms.

Families are welcome in the dining areas and dogs on a lead in the bar only.

Weekday opening times Monday–Thursday 11–3 and 5.30–11. Friday, Saturday and Sunday open all day 11–11.

Telephone: 01435 872200.

The lovely village of Mayfield is on the A267 between Eastbourne and Tunbridge Wells. Continue east through the village and down the hill to the road junction. The pub is on the left.

Approx. distance of walk: 3½ mile. O.S.Map No. 188 TQ 592/272.

There is ample car parking both at the side, the front and in the lane.

A very enjoyable but fairly demanding walk mostly across farm land and through woods which twice crosses a tributary of the Rother. Strong waterproof footwear is to be recommended in the winter.

1. Leave the pub turning right then immediately left into East Street walking down the hill in the direction of Broad Oak. Further on turn left into Southmead Close, walk round to the right until you reach a short track on the left between two houses leading to a farm gate. Just before the gate turn right onto the footpath behind the houses, pass through the gate, into the field and across to the stile opposite then through the trees. Ignoring the stile on the right, keep straight ahead beside the hedge down to the bottom of the field following the path into the wood.

2. Further ahead go over the crossing into the adjoining field and turn left walking down until you reach the crossing point on the left. Re-enter the woods and bear half right following the twisting path as best you can down through the trees to the wooden bridge. Cross the stream into the field and keep straight ahead, past the building and up to the stile. Continue in the same direction crossing two more stiles before entering the driveway then turn right, soon to turn left onto the farm road following it up to the lane.

3. Walk straight across into Lake Street and keep going until you eventually reach a stile on the left opposite the entrance to the lodge. Go over onto the manicured lawn and bear half left making your way down to the gate and stile at the bottom. Cross the brook, walk up to the stile, go into the field and turn left. Keeping close to the hedge head down the field to the gap at the bottom maintaining direction until you reach the stile on the left.

4. Go over into the trees and bear right, cross the plank bridge and up into the field turning left. Keep straight ahead through the gate walking fairly close to the hedge on the left. Pass into the field ahead and aim for the gap opposite. Continue in the same direction into the next field finally walking down to the wooden crossing point at the bottom before the bridge. Cross the river and maintain your direction following the path up through the trees. Although not well defined the higher you climb the more obvious it becomes. Eventually when you enter a field, keep straight ahead over the crossing points walking to the top then turn left over the cattle grid making for the stile ahead turning right into the lane back to the pub.

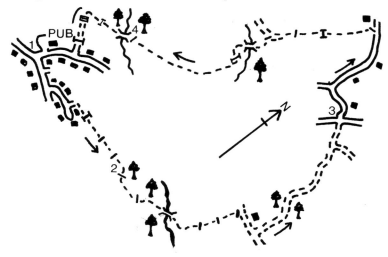

The Sussex Ox, Milton Street

The ideal walkers' pub must preferably be sited in a remote scenic spot, be simply furnished but comfortable, have a warm welcoming relaxed atmosphere, serve good food and well kept real ale. Such was my delight when I entered Milton Street for the first time and found The Sussex Ox. Originally a butcher's shop it became a pub some eighty years ago. Today the bare and boarded floor, the open fireplace and the painted boarded walls and ceiling of the main bar all add to the rustic charm. A stable door allows access to the comfortably furnished 'Sty' family room whilst diners can choose to sit in the 'Harness Room' restaurant. Outside there is a large garden and play area.

The inn is a freehouse very well run by the new owner Douglas Baker. Two regular real ales include Harvey's Best Bitter and Hopback Summer Lightning.

Excellent food, freshly prepared by the same chef for a number of years, is served seven days a week 11–2 and 6–9, Sunday 12–2 and 6–9 with afternoon snacks. From the set menu, which changes between winter and summer, starters can range from pan fried king prawns to a hot seafood dip followed by garlic and herb chicken, the pub's own recipe Sussex Ox burger, cheese topped cottage pie and country ploughman's. Specials are chalked daily on the blackboard and I could have chosen homemade vegetable soup, creamy garlic mushrooms followed by steak, ale and mushroom pie. Fish dishes included dressed crab, smoked trout pate, moules mariniere and homemade mariners pot. There were two vegetarian dishes, vegetable hot pot and broccoli and Stilton quiche whilst sweets ranged from bread and butter pudding to rhubarb and orange crumble.

There is no accommodation but camping is permitted.

Children are welcome in all but the main bar and there is no objection to dogs on a lead in the bar but not the restaurant.

Weekday opening times are from 11–3 and 6–11. Sunday all day 12–10.30. Telephone: 01323 870840.

Village signed south from the A27, 2 miles west of Polegate.

Approx. distance of walk: 3 miles. O.S.Map No 199 TQ 534/039.

On road parking is fairly restricted but there is a large car park at the pub.

A short but nevertheless very enjoyable, scenic walk at first along the banks of the Cuckmere River then onto The South Downs Way walking high up on to Wilmington Down. Mostly good underfoot and not over strenuous makes it an ideal walk for all the family.

1. Turn right from the pub walking down hill in the direction of Alfriston shortly to reach a stile on the left. Go over into the field and head down in the direction of the arrow towards the stile in the bottom hedge. Turn left into the lane walking until you reach the kissing gate on the right. After cutting the corner a similar kissing gate allows you to exit into the lane by the bridge. Cross the river and immediately take the stile on the left. Keep to the raised path beside the Cuckmere crossing a couple of stiles before reaching the bridge at Alfriston. One of England's oldest villages inhabited first by The Saxons and later by The Normans, is today a popular tourist destination.
2. Cross to the far side and follow the little path up to the lane and turn right at Plonk Barn. Almost Immediately join the signed footpath on the left and, in a couple of hundred yards, cross the stile into the field on the left leading to the South Downs Way. The well trodden path steadily rises to a stile and continues up the field to the stile in the hedge at the top meeting the track.
3. Turn right, cross the lane to the gate opposite and make you way up Wilmington Hill on the bridleway. Pass through the gate and turn left heading down the hillside making for the small wooden gate at the bottom. Fork left to the road, cross over and take the bridleway signed to Milton Street. Take care as you go the surface can be quite uneven in places and slippery in winter. Fork left at the bottom back to the pub.

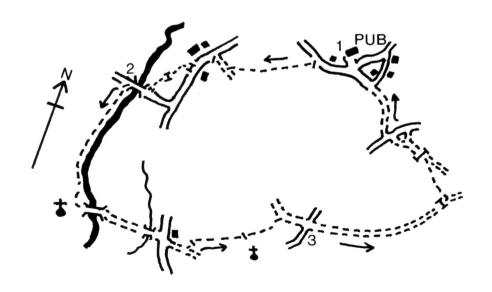

Star Inn, Old Heathfield

Any book featuring East Sussex pubs would be incomplete without the charming Star Inn. Built in 1348 to house the masons, building All Saints Church, later in 1388, with the consent of the church, the hostel became an alehouse known as The Starre. Beyond the solid stone exterior the unspoilt main bar of this ancient inn has a heavily beamed ceiling, part panelled walls and a massive inglenook fireplace with a warm log fire in winter, whilst the timeless 'Tap Bar' has a low ceiling, an old fireplace with a raised hearth, painted, boarded walls and intimate high back wooden settles. A short staircase leads up to a delightful atmospheric restaurant, which has paintings on the curved ceiling and a fireplace in the sidewall. Outside there are picnic tables in the pretty award winning front garden.

The inn is a freehouse now well run by Fiona Airey. On offer is a choice of very well kept real ales, two regulars, Harvey's Sussex Best and King and Barnes Sussex Bitter sit along side a guest ale such as the delightful Summer Lightning from the Hop Back Brewery in Salisbury.

Exceptionally good food is available every day 12–2.15 and 7–9.30, weekends 12–2.30. The constantly changing menus, prepared by the same chef for a number of years, are chalked on various blackboards and could include delicious homemade soups, chef's pate, home-cooked ham and eggs, chicken poached in white wine, steak and ale pie and a 12-oz Scottish sirloin steak. Fish is prominent on the restaurant menu which on my last visit listed a pint of prawns and roll mop salad followed by fresh crab, poached salmon steak, lobster with garlic butter, fresh mussels with garlic, onions, cream, wine and saffron plus one dozen marinated Belgian anchovy fillets.

Families are welcome and well-behaved dogs on leads.

Weekday opening times are from 11.30–3 and 5.30 (6.30 in winter)–11, Sunday all day 12–10.30

Telephone: 01435 863570

The village is west of Heathfield signed from the B2203 and the B2096.

Approx. distance of walk: 3 miles. O.S.Map No.199 TQ 598/203.

Parking is limited to the car park at the front or in the lane leading to the pub.

One of my favourite East Sussex walks from one of my favourite pubs, at first across farm land then through attractive woods and along shaded paths fringed with wild flowers. After passing through a delightful bluebell wood the path runs close to the grounds of Nettlesworth Place then skirts woodland crossing meadow land back to the pub. Be warned though it can sometimes be very muddy during periods of bad weather.

1. Leave the pub and walk down the lane at the front until you come to a stile on the right then go into the field and make your way over to the kissing gates either side of the drive. Keeping to the headland walk down the field to the stile at the bottom, cross the road, pass through the gate opposite and follow the shaded path down between the fields to the stile then turn left.

2. Keep to the field boundary beside the hedge then cross the bridge. Further ahead the footpath has recently collapsed and for now you must divert down to the stream. After climbing the rise the path widens and levels out passing a lake on the right. Keep walking until you reach the field boundary then fork right, round to the gate, through onto the track and turn left.

3. After passing the cottage maintain direction into the field, step over the stream, cross the stile and keep straight ahead at the finger post. At the stile cross over onto the shaded path and keep walking until you reach the next finger post then turn left. Further ahead cross the track, and the stile, and enter the bluebell wood. It is very attractive planted mostly with beech and coppiced chestnut. Leave by the stile and follow the path through the trees, past the farm house and lake to join the drive up to the road.

4. Walk straight across into the lane opposite and turn left when you reach the track. Keep to the side of the woods until a path sign directs you through the gate into the field on the left. Make your way down and across to the far corner, over the stream and onto the track ahead. Walk round soon to reach the stile on the right then cross into the field and head for the stile at the top. Follow the hedge boundary round, past the front of the house, through the kissing gate into the field ahead and continue round, through one last farm gate, back to the kissing gates, retracing your steps to the pub.

The attractive garden at the Star

A view from the walk close to the village

The Two Sawyers, Pett

In typical Sussex style the Two Sawyers is a combination of an old ale house, butchers shop and forge, part of which dates back to the 15th century. Both attractive unspoilt bars have low-beamed ceilings and large fireplaces one with an inglenook log fire. There is a seventy-six seater restaurant and outside a pretty sheltered beer garden and a boules pitch.

The inn is a freehouse well run by the new owners Clive Soper and John and Karen Perkins. Five real ales include three from their own brewery plus two others from small independent breweries. Additionally there is a choice of over twenty wines from around the world.

A large menu with many tempting dishes is available daily 12–2.30 and 6.30–9.30 (Sunday 7–9). In addition to specials like wild boar served with roasted peppers, topped with a honey and whisky sauce, starters range from prawn pil pil and New Zealand green lipped mussels to sardines á la fromage and deep-fried calamari. Main courses listed on the menu include favourites such as home-made beef, mushroom and ale pie and homemade liver and bacon casserole. There is a filleted duck breast served with a rich orange sauce and a brace of their butcher's large grilled pork chops. A choice of sizzling dishes include crocodile with mixed peppers whilst curry lovers have a choice of four. Others dishes listed are a large locally caught cod served in the chef's own traditional beer batter and pan fried and flambé fresh local sea bass in a ginger and Pernod sauce. Vegetarians are well catered for with dishes like pancakes stuffed with asparagus and topped with a mushroom and brandy sauce.

Children have their own comprehensive menu and a wide choice of sweets are on offer for the pudding lovers.

Accommodation is in six rooms, which includes a family room for up to six.

Families and dogs both equally welcome.

Opening times Monday to Thursday all day 11–11, Friday and Saturday 11–12 and Sunday 11–10.30.

Telephone: 01424 812255. Fax: 813928. email: clive@twosawyers.com.

Walk No. 27

Village signed east from the A259 Hastings to Rye road.

Approx. distance of walk: 2 miles O.S.Map No 199 TQ 866/136.

Park in the car park or in the lane outside.

Although short this very enjoyable, scenic ramble at first descends through an attractive bluebell wood to a peaceful country lane with some pretty cottage returning across rolling farm land. The going is mostly good underfoot making it ideal for all the family.

1. Walk straight across the road to the signed footpath opposite and enter the blue-bell wood. Leave by the stile at the bottom and bear right across the field making for the metal gate beside the barn then keep straight across the field to the stile, go out into the lane turning left.

2. After walking past some attractive cottages and just beyond the bridge go through the gate on the left and follow the signed footpath up the field in the direction of the finger post making for the stile in the hedge. Continue in the same direction across to the gate on the far side, go through and bear right towards the hedge following it down to the bridge.

3. Cross the stream into the field ahead and make your way up to the stile in the top corner. Follow the path through the trees to the stile and up into the field. Continue climbing negotiating a couple more stiles then bear left across the field to one last stile before joining the path next to the church leading up to the lane.

4. Turn left, cross the road, and if you are not desperate for a drink, in twenty paces take the signed footpath between the houses. After entering the field bear half left across to the far corner and go through the gap into the field then across to the stile.

Take the left field path to the stile and join the narrow path behind the rear gardens of the houses. After one last stile keep straight ahead onto the gravel drive leading up to the road then turn right back to the pub.

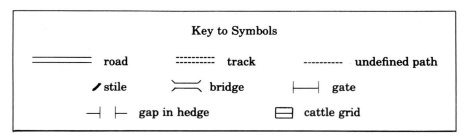

Key to Symbols

======= road   ---------- track   ---------- undefined path

✔ stile   ⟩—⟨ bridge   ⊢—⊣ gate

⊣ ⊢ gap in hedge   ⊟ cattle grid

66

The Half Moon, Plumpton

Until the turn of the century The Half Moon, built in 1842, served as a coaching stop on the Ditchling to Ofham turnpike. Today the main bar of the mostly open plan interior has a comfortably partioned dining area at one end and a games room the other. In the centre, close to the bar, is an attractive brick fireplace with warm log fire in winter. One interesting feature in the bar is a large painting, one and a half feet by three feet, which depicts one hundred and thirty happy regulars which took the artist, Dick Leech, three months to paint in 1978. Outside at the front are flower-covered pergolas with seating plus many more picnic benches in the attractive back garden where there is also a very good children's play area.

The pub last changed hands in March 2001 and is now owned by Chris Symes and Gavin Young. Presently there are three real ales Harvery's Bitter, Morland Old Speckled Hen and Charles Wells Bombardier Premium Bitter.

Bar food is served seven days a week 12–2.30 and 6.30–9, the menu chalked daily on the blackboards. Apart from jacket potatoes and ploughman's there is a choice of dishes such as Homity pie made with bacon, onions, potatoes and cheese, steak and mushroom pie. Also vegetarian lasagne, macaroni cheese and Stilton and mushroom quiche. The majority of dishes are homemade and where that is so they are marked with an asterisk. Additional evening specials include assorted steaks, roast duck with orange or black cherry sauce, homemade chicken chasseur and sweet and sour pork. Sweets range from homemade treacle tart and banoffi pie to bread and butter pudding and apple and mincemeat crumble.

Children are welcome and dogs too on a lead.

Weekday opening times are from 12–3 and 6–11.30.

Telephone: 01273 890253.

Walk No. 28

Plumpton is situated on the B2116 about 4 miles west of Lewes.

Approx. distance of walk: 3½ miles. O.S Map No.198 TQ 364/133.

There is a large car park at the rear of the pub also space for parking in Plumpton Lane at the side.

A very enjoyable scenic walk which takes you high up onto the South Downs Way returning through the grounds of Novington Manor. The going is mostly good underfoot but the climb up onto the downs can be quite strenuous.

1. Turn left from the inn, cross the road and in twenty paces join the bridleway signed to Plumpton Plain. Follow the attractive, wild flower lined track as it rises steadily before reaching a gate on the left. Go through and climb the hillside in the direction of the arrow taking time to look back and admire the view. Eventually when you reach the top you will find a small gate in the fence which takes you though onto The South Downs Way then turn left.

2. Proceed forward and when you reach the large gate go through and turn left following the track beside the woods, round to the right and down only as far as the track on the left. Take this track following it steadily down through the woods until you reach the finger post then fork right on to the narrow path down through the trees to the road at the bottom. It is an attractive path quite steep at times but there are steps on the most demanding section.

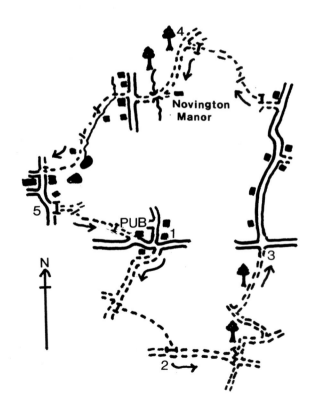

68

3. Carefully cross over into Norrington Lane and in about three quarters of a mile look for a short track beside a house on the left leading to a stile. Go over into the field and bear right making you way across to the stiles in the right-hand hedge. Turn half left, cross the plank bridge and continue in the same direction towards the stile beside the gate, go over onto the track and turn left.

4. After passing private woodland, carpeted white in spring with wood anemones, cross the stile and turn right down the drive of Novington Manor, out into the lane and straight across onto the signed footpath beside the post box. Climb the stile into the field and bear left over to the stile in the bottom hedge. Cross the plank bridge and immediately turn left following the path close to the stream. Pass through the gap in the hedge and maintain your direction to the stile in the far hedge. After negotiating the plank bridge cross the field to the far-side, past the ornamental lakes onto the path leading into the plantation. Walk round to the right and when you reach the wooden gate in the high fence go through into the grounds of the Agricultural College turning left.

5. After passing the main buildings, and just beyond the end of the wooden fence on the left, go through the gate into the field on the left, and further ahead cross the stile into the field on the right, then bear right following the well trodden path across to the stile on the far side back to the pub.

The view north from the downs above Plumpton

The Cock, Ringmer

Since the main road was upgraded and the bends straightened out the only traffic that now approaches The Cock are people seeking out the excellent hospitality. High above the road and backing onto open fields the pub looks resplendent its white weather boarded front making the perfect back drop for the many hanging flower baskets and window boxes. Inside a warm and cosy atmosphere pervades in the low, heavily beamed main bar comfortably furnished with wooden settles and sturdy farmhouse tables and where a warm log fire crackles in the large iglenook fireplace. There is a separate room for non-smokers and an attractive restaurant. Summer barbecues are a feature in the large beer garden and there are seats on the sunny front terrace.

Originally owned by Tamplins it eventually became part of Grand Met, but is now leased to John and Joy Garnsey the long-standing tenants who run it as a freehouse. Presently there are four real ales, London Pride, Rother Valley Spirit Level, Harvey's Best and for the summer Harvey's Mild and for the winter Harvey's Old Ale.

A good choice of excellent bar food, freshly prepared to order, is available from 6.30 in the evening. The menu, designed to cater for all tastes and chalked daily on the blackboard, offers a choice of starters like fresh sardines and red peppers stuffed with sun dried tomatoes, mushrooms and goats cheese. Followed by chicken Florentina—chicken cooked with spinach in a cheese sauce topped with melted Cheddar, steak and ale pie, lamb chops in garlic and rosemary and ham and eggs. Vegetarians have the choice of crunchy pasta bake, vegetable curry or spinach, chestnut and ricotta parcels served with red wine sauce whilst the sweet toothed can plump for homemade pavlova or sticky toffee, date and walnut pudding.

Weekday opening times 11–3 and 6–11, usual Sunday hours.

Well controlled dogs are welcome and children away from the bar.

Telephone: 01273 812040

Pub located just off the A26 about 2 miles north from Lewes.

Approx. distance of walk: 1½ miles. O.S. Map No 198 TQ 439/137.

Park anywhere at the front.

An ideal family walk short but nevertheless enjoyable across open fields and along peaceful country lanes.

1. From the pub turn right and in twenty paces take the signed footpath on the right. Cross the stile into the field and keep straight ahead towards the gateway in the wire fence. Continue in the same direction to a gap in the far hedge and then make for the right-hand side of the farm buildings where you will find a stile leading out into the lane.

2. Turn left following the lane round for just under half a mile at which point you will you will see a signed footpath on the left opposite Wellingham House. Cross the fence into the field and bear slightly left to the pair of stiles and ditch then bear right up the rise, through a couple more fields before reaching the stile by the farm buildings. Make your way left across to the track and turn right. Go out into the road turning left eventually reaching the pub.

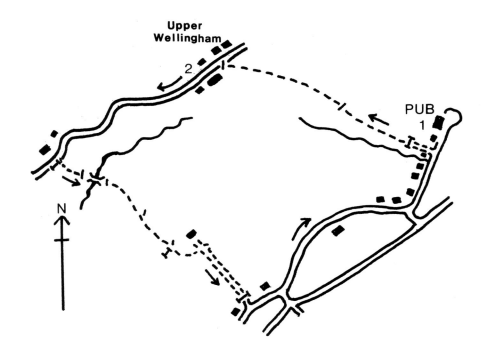

Horse & Groom, Rushlake Green

The largely unspoilt Horse & Groom, originally a 16th century farm house, occupies an enviable position overlooking the village green where cricketers have now given way to the ducks. The main bar has a low-beamed ceiling, sensibly padded at the lowest point, and an open fire in winter. A wooden screen separates the 'saddle room' from which a door leads out onto the back terrace and bench filled beer gardens. Diners may prefer to sit in the equally attractive 'Gun Room' restaurant also heavily beamed and heated by a log fire in the big hearth. A gun collection is displayed on the walls whilst lots of old photographs hang in the main bar. The earliest is a picture of the pub taken in 1858. There are picnic benches in the front garden with more seating in the recently enlarged rear gardens.

The inn is a freehouse lovingly cared for and personally run by the owners Mike and Sue Chappell who only took over recently. Presently there are three well kept real ales Harveys Best and two from Shepherd & Neame, Spitfire Premium Ale and Master Brew Bitter.

Very good home-cooked food is served seven days a week 12–12.15 and 7–9.15. Snacks available in the bar include sandwiches, jacket potatoes and ploughman's plus the usual pub favourites like pies and scampi etc. but for those wanting something more substantial an excellent menu is displayed on the blackboard by the entrance. Fresh fish dishes are the speciality, changed on a regular basis they can include grilled sea bass, Dover sole or dishes like fillets of monkfish wrapped in Parmesan ham and served on a bed of ratatouille with a sweet pepper sauce. An alternative dish might include marinated duck breast on oriental stir fried vegetables with a Riesling and Marsala sauce. Vegetarians can choose between a couple of dishes but the chef is always prepared to cater for special dietary needs.

Families are welcome and there is no objection to well behaved dogs.

Weekday opening times 11.30–3 and 5.30–11.

Telephone: 01435 830320.

The village is situated west of Heathfield, best reached south from the B2096 at Three Cups Corner.

Approx. distance of walk: 3 miles. O.S.Map No.199 TQ 627/185.

Park anywhere around the green.

A very enjoyable but fairly challenging walk along peaceful country lanes, across farm land, over streams and through bluebell woods.

1. Turn left from the pub, then right and second left, signed to Woods Corner. Follow the attractive lane as it rises steadily before reaching a stile beside a metal farm gate on the left. Go over into the field making for the stile in the opposite fence and the gap in the far hedge. Keeping close to the hedge walk down the field to the stream, cross the stile and plank bridge, climb the bank to the stile and turn left leaving the field by the gate.

2. Cross the lane, pass through the gate into the field walking down to the bottom. Carefully climb into the field on the right and turn left continuing down to the gate on the left of the barn, over the stile into the lane and turn right.

3. Either keep to the lane walking to the top of the hill or divert through a bluebell wood by turning right at the next bend before the bridge. Follow the signed path into the field then take the stile on the left just before reaching the gate. Walk down the path into Kemp's Wood then up into the field and back to the lane. At times it can be very wet and become overgrown making the exact path a bit difficult to follow.

4. After passing a dwelling on the left, but just before the bend, there is a short track on the left leading into a field beside which is a footpath. Take this path down to the crossing point and into the field bearing left across to the stile in the far left-hand corner which leads down to a bridge in the centre of a beautiful bluebell copse. Climb the bank, enter the field and head straight across to the gap in the hedge opposite.

5. Cross the lane onto the path beside the garage, walk round the garden and head for the corner of the field. Go through the hedge and turn right across the corner of the field making for the gap in the hedge opposite the barn turning left into the lane.

6. After about a third of a mile you come to a field entrance on the left opposite a bridleway, look for the footpath stone on the left. Enter the field keeping to the track, cross the open field and head for the path down into the trees. Cross the bridge and climb the fenced path on the far side to the stile at the top, through the garden back to the pub.

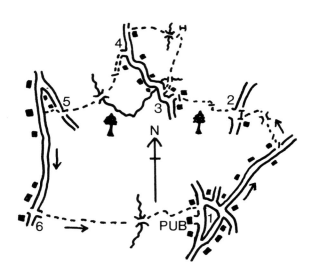

The Mermaid Inn, Rye

One of the ancient Cinque Ports, Rye is a beautiful town with many of its old cobbled streets and buildings surviving today. Instantly noticeable are the tall wooden buildings by the quay used by fisherman to hang their nets. Rye Castle, built in 1249 to house prisoners, is now a museum and The Landgate is considered to be the finest of its kind in Southern England.

The very lovely, black and white timbered Mermaid, which probably dates from 1156 but rebuilt in 1420, is one of England's oldest inns and has unique connections with the days of smuggling. Ships timbers were used in the construction with wood salvaged from French ships carved to make the fireplaces. The aptly named ancient 'parlour and fireplace' bar has a heavily timbered and boarded ceiling and a massive step-in fireplace the entire length of one wall housing a roaring log fire in winter. Assorted furnishings include several interesting antique seats one of them carved in the form of a goat. On the other side of the coach arch candles top the tables in the large, heavily timbered restaurant and there is some seating outside at the back. Classical background music.

The inn is a freehouse presently offering well conditioned Morland Old Speckled Hen, a section of malt whiskies and cognacs.

Food can be ordered every day 12–2.15 and 7–10.30. Bar food offers a good selection from their specialty 'Mermaid' seafood platter and moules mariniere, with popular homemade steak and kidney pudding on their winter menu, through to a selection of baguettes, freshly made to order. For those wishing to dine in their famous, panelled, rosette restaurant the table d'hote menu lists a tasty pan fried crab cake and oak smoked chicken Caesar salad followed by fillets of plaice francaise, sauté calves liver and confit of duck. Whilst from the à la carte menu one could choose pressed terrine of fois gras or a warm smoked quail salad plus pot roast partridge and the Mermaid's fruit de mer.

Families are welcome but no dogs inside.

A good choice of accommodation is available ranging from four-poster and double bedrooms to single and family rooms. There is 24-hour porterage.

The inn is open all day from 11.

Telephone: 01797 223065. Fax: 225069. www.mermaidinn.com

The historic town of Rye lies close to the Kent/Sussex border on the A259 between Hastings and Folkestone. The inn is near the top of Mermaid Street.

Approx. distance of walk: 4½ miles. O.S. Map No. 189 TQ 921/202.

Parking is very limited at the inn, it is best to use one of the 'pay and display' car parks at the bottom of Mermaid Street near the Tourist Information Centre.

A most enjoyable ramble from this attractive old town. The twisting cobbled street of this once prosperous sea port undulates inland affording delightful views along the Tillingham valley and across the marshy levels of Walland and Romney Marsh. The well marked paths and tracks are generally good underfoot.

1. Leave the inn turning left shortly to turn right at the T junction with West Street. Keep left on entering Church Square and follow the footpath soon to turn left down Lion Street. Turn right into Market Street and upon reaching the High Street cross over into Conduit Hill and pass Iden Pottery. Keep straight ahead at the crossroads along Rope Walk, cross the railway line and bear left with Love Lane passing the college.

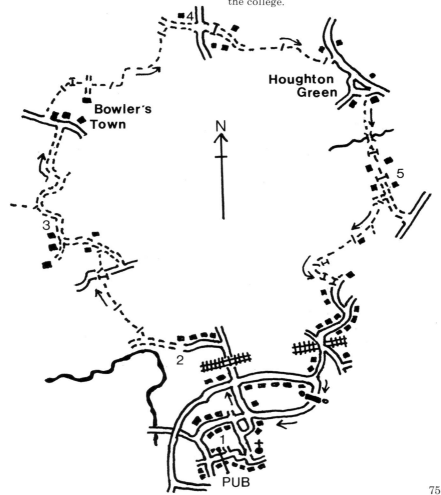

75

2. At the end of the lane proceed ahead along a track - river to your left - towards a farmhouse. Climb the stile in front of the house and gradually ascend the grassy hill with good views to a waymarked stile. Continue alongside an old field boundary, pass through a metal gate and cross a private drive (fingerpost) and a stile to join a defined path through trees to a further stile. Turn left onto a track and follow it through a farmyard soon to bear right in front of a converted oasthouse, then keep right of Leasam Oast Cottage onto a wide grass centered track.

3. Keep left with the old sunken track downhill, disregard arrowed path left and proceed along the edge of a field. In the corner bear off left on a narrow path down a bank to join a further grassy track that keeps left-handed through fields, gently uphill to the A268 in Bowlers Town. Turn left then almost immediately cross over to take the waymarked path in the field beside a weatherboarded cottage. Keep right-handed, climb a stile and turn right through a gate then keep to left-hand edge of a field towards a farmyard. Proceed across a track and climb a stile hidden in a hedgerow into an orchard. Turn left, then shortly right along a wide grassy gap between trees to the orchard fringe. Turn left and look for a stile on your right (can be overgrown) then bear right opposite a house along its gravel drive to the B2082.

4. Cross over, pass through a gate and follow the driveway, soon to bear left in front of a brick and black weatherboarded outbuilding and shortly enter a field, climb a waymarked stile and keep left-handed through pasture to a stile in the field corner and a lane. Turn right, then next right (Houghton Green) uphill to a T junction of lanes. Bear slightly left, cross over to join an arrowed path between fencing and houses eventually reaching a stile. Proceed ahead in the direction of fingerpost downhill through an open field towards farm buildings. Cross a brook and soon pass through two gates onto a track.

5. Shortly bear right (yellow arrow) and climb stile beside driveway to 'Saltbarn'. Keep left along fence, cross pasture to wire fencing and a junction of paths at a waymarked post. Proceed right along the fence to a stile, then continue uphill through pasture to an arrowed stile beside a stile. Bear diagonally left downhill, pass through two small wooden gates and turn right along a tarmac drive downhill to a road. Turn right along footway into Rye. Keep left at T junction, cross the railway bridge and soon bear off left up Landgate to pass beneath the old fort back into the town centre retracing your steps to the Mermaid.

Other Local Publications

Available direct from the publishers or from your local bookshop.

One of many cobbled streets in Rye

Powdermill Reservoir

The Queens Head, Sedlescombe

Originally the property of The Abbot of Battle and first registered as a trading house in 1523 this old coaching inn was the turning point for the Eastbourne run. There are stables at the back and an ancient horse trough is still in place at the side. Today this very attractive pub, set back from the village road behind a small green, has a red bricked and tile hung exterior under a Sussex tiled roof. Hanging from the low-beamed ceiling of the comfortably furnished and beautifully kept bar are lots of mugs and garlands of hops whilst paintings decorate the walls. A warm log fires heats the bar in winter. Old farming implements are displayed in the sunny, flower filled front garden whilst there are picnic benches in the lawned beer garden at the side and an aviary of interest to children.

The inn, originally a Whitbread pub last changed hands in 2001. You can take your pick from at least three real ales like Flowers Original, local Harvey's Best Bitter and Youngs Bitter.

Food is available 12–2.30 and 6–9.30 except Monday evening. Typical pub food includes dishes with chips, giant Yorkshire pudding, lasagne, hearty Ploughman's, freshly cut sandwiches and warming soups for the winter months.

Well behaved dogs and children welcome.

Weekday opening times all day 11–11, Sunday 12–10.30.

Telephone: 01424 870228.

Pub is on the A229 set back from the road behind a green.

Approx. distance of walk: 4½ miles. O.S.Map No. 199 TQ 782/179.

Park anywhere in the lane outside the pub.

A slightly demanding but very enjoyable walk at first down a peaceful country lane and then on woodland paths with glimpses of Powdermill Reservoir before returning across farm land and on well established tracks.

1. Turn right from the pub and go up the lane past the newly built houses walking for about a mile until you reach the stile ahead of you just before the bend. Go over into the field and cross to the stile in the far corner entering the lane by the entrance to Jacob's Farm. Turn left and continue down the lane and after passing a house look for a stile on the left.

2. Follow the path up through the trees then cross a second stile on the right. The slightly obscure path winds its way through a new plantation of trees before reaching a stile allowing access to an open area of scrub. On the right you get a lovely view down to the reservoir. After reaching the crossing point descend to the bridge and climb the steps into the wood. Having crossed a ditch the path rises up to a stile in the fence. Bearing right walk across the open ground to the stile opposite and enter the woods.

3. After a short distance look for a path on the left indicated by a low marker post. It is a very attractive path winding its way through woods and across the occasional bridge. Upon reaching the grassy path bear, left then left again on to the wide forest track. When you reach the farm gate cross into the field and keep straight ahead to the far side. Enter the field on the left and continue walking up beside the hedge to the stile, go over onto the path and up to the lane.

4. Walk straight across and join the signed path opposite. When you reach the gravel road turn right and continue walking past the dwellings on to the grassy track, which narrows to a path and enters a field. Leave by the stile onto the concrete road turning left in to the gravel lane, down to the main road and left again back to the pub.

The Peacock Inn, Shortbridge

Set back from the road in a high sunny position and fronted by two, two-hundred year old yew trees, this lovely old 17th century pub has a white and black boarded front under a tiled roof. The lovely unspoilt interior has a low, heavily beamed ceiling, part wood panelled walls, an attractive carved wooden bar and a huge inglenook fireplace with crackling logs in a raised grate. Furnishings consist of simple farmhouse tables and chairs on a plain floor. A similar but more comfortable dining room is serviced by a hatch in the wall from which a door leads out to the attractive back garden where there is a children's play area and summer barbecue with more seating on the sunny front terrace.

The inn is a freehouse personally run by the owner Matthew Arnold, himself a qualified chef. There is usually a choice of five real ales, which might include Boddingtons Bitter, Flowers Original, Harveys Best, Marston's Pedigree and Old Speckled Hen.

Very good, home-cooked food is served seven days a week. Daily specials such as fresh plaice and escallop of pork in a cider, honey and cream sauce supplement the bar menu which lists 'Shortbridge' pie consisting of tender pieces of chicken and leeks in a Stilton sauce, hot chilli pancake and broccoli, spinach and flaked almond pancake. There are various curries, chicken lasagne in brandy sauce also the usual snacks like jacket potatoes, sandwiches and ploughman's plus a separate children's menu. The restaurant, open till midnight, offers a full à la carte menu featuring ten starters alone like Boursin cheese wrapped in filo pastry, oven baked and served on a gooseberry sauce and Sussex smokies—smoked haddock in a cream sauce topped with cheese and bread crumbs followed by 'Peacock chicken' which is the breast with cashew nuts in a bacon, garlic and cream sauce and for vegetarians stir fried vegetable stroganoff.

Families and dogs are equally welcome.

Weekday opening times all day 11–11. Teas served between 3 and 6.

Telephone: 01825 762463.

Village is just south from the A272 between Nerwick and Maresfield.

Approx. distance of walk: 3 miles. O.S.Map No. 198 TQ 450/215.

Park at the front or in the large car park opposite.

An enjoyable ramble at first along the banks of a tributary of the Ouse, then across farm land and a golf course back to the pub. Although not a long walk it can be very muddy in places in winter making slow going; the best time would be late spring or summer. The award winning 35 acre vineyard is open to the public from Apr–Dec 24th 10 a.m. to 5 p.m., Tue–Sat 11 a.m. to 5 p.m., Sundays and Bank Holidays.

1. Turn right from the pub, cross the bridge and fork right in the direction of Lewes. Almost immediately cross the stile into the field on the right and head for the gate opposite. Bear left across the lawn, up to the wooden gates and onto the track ahead. The path follows a line fairly close to the river moving occasionally from lower to higher ground avoiding the often boggy conditions. It is very attractive in late spring and summer carpeted with numerous wild flowers. Climb the crossing point and continue following the riverbank over a couple more stiles and then divert across the field making for the bridge in the distance. Cross the Ouse and bear right over to the stile in the hedge and continue in the same direction up to the stile beside the gate, go out into the lane and turn right.

2. After crossing the river and just beyond an attractive timber clad house climb the stile into the field on the left and bear half right across to the stile, over into the field bearing right in the direction of the arrow. At the top of the field turn right over the plank bridge and follow the wide grass strip round the vineyard until you reach a farm gate on the left into the pig farm. Unless you want to visit the vineyard follow the fenced path up to the main road and turn right soon to reach bridleway 32 running down beside Stonecroft Cottages. Negotiable with care it shortly meets the lane then turn left.

3. Turn right at the road junction and further ahead turn left onto the golf course which hopefully has now been signed. The footpath follows a line parallel with woods and a private property on the right, across a fairway and into scrub on the far side, beyond which is a gateway leading into a field. From here turn left walking down the headland until you reach a gap in the hedge then cross the stream beside the stone footpath marker and turn right on to the drive leading back to the pub.

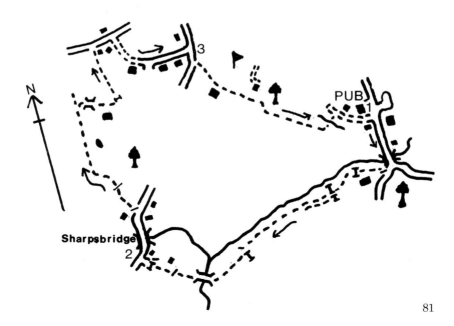

The Bull (Three Legged Cross), Ticehurst

Nestling in a tiny hamlet close to the Bewel Bridge Reservoir this lovely old pub, built around a Wealden Hall House, was constructed between 1385 and 1425. The ancient beamed ceilings and timber framed walls, in-filled with wattle-and-daub, still survive today. Furniture consists of an assortment of long wooden tables, pew bench seats and kitchen chairs. The floor is either flagged, brick or parquet and both rooms have large open fireplaces with warm log fires in winter. There is a separate very attractive dining room built in similar style and a lovely beer garden with an ornamental fish pond and two petanque pitches.

The inn is a freehouse presently offering four real ales Harvey's Best, Level Best, draught Bass and Bull Best plus a range of lagers and cider.

An interesting choice of food is available weekday 12–2.30 (Saturday & Sunday 3) and 6.30–9.30 (Sunday 9). Apart from daily specials like beef and ale pie and aubergine brasque, starters on the à la carte menu range from homemade soup coquille St Jacques to Bull special–lardons of bacon, button mushrooms and prawns sautéed in garlic butter and spanakopitta–spinach and feta cheese with herbs and spices in filo pastry parcels. Rack of lamb heads the list of main courses followed by various steaks, New York chicken, Barbury duck breast, country mixed grill and pollo saperitorlic–chicken breast in olive oil, garlic and bacon, garnished with black olives and served on a bed of tagliatelle with salad. Fish lovers and vegetarians are well catered for with dishes such as Champagne Dover sole and a vegetable jambalaya, followed by homemade desserts and a bottomless cup of coffee.

Opening times all day 11–11 Sunday 12–10.30.

Children are welcome in the dining area and dogs in the bar on a lead.

Four en-suite rooms with bed and breakfast.

Telephone: 01580 200586. Fax: 201289. www.thebullinn.co.uk.

Entering Ticehurst from the B2099 take the turning north signed to Three Legged Cross (also known as Three Leg Cross). The inn is on the left about a quarter of a mile down the lane.

Approx. distance of walk: $2\frac{1}{4}$ miles O.S.Map No 188 TQ 685/311.

Although there is ample parking at the pub you can safely park in the lane outside.

A short but very enjoyable and peaceful ramble down to Bewel Water, the largest area of inland water in South East England. Apart from the occasional muddy patch it is mostly good underfoot making it ideal for all the family.

1. Turn left from the pub walk up the lane forking left. Look for the signed footpath on the left then turn onto the tarred drive bearing right on the road to Hazelhurst Farm. Just before reaching the cattle grid there is a wooden gate on the left allowing access to the bridleway. Pass through following it down to the next gate, straight ahead across the ditch, around the estuary and back towards the point passing through a gate on the way.

2. When you reach the headland turn back inland through the gate on to the grassy path. After passing through a couple more gates the path widens to become a tarred lane. Take the first turning left past the dwelling and left again at the road junction. After a steady climb for about half a mile you will arrive back at the pub.

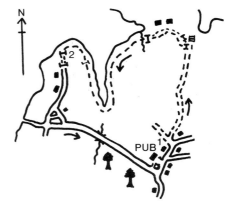

Bewel Bridge Reservoir

The Plough, Upper Dicker

Originally a farmhouse dating from 1641 The Plough was last refurbished in 2000. There are now two bars, one is in the old dining room with an inglenook fireplace and open fire the other where the original stove was. Two restaurants have been added and there are 'The Stables' where families may eat and the lower dining room, which along with the lower bar is childfree. The garden extends to an acre having a children's play area, boules pitch and horseshoe toss. Excellent wheel chair facilities. No live music, background only.

The pub, now owned by Shepherd and Neame and well run by Glenn and Helen serves their Best Bitter, Spitfire and Bishops Finger traditionally straight from the cask.

A lunch menu is served everyday between 12 and 2.30. In addition to ploughman's, dishes range from bacon and onion pudding and ham, leek and potato pie to goats cheese and spinach lasagne and Sussex smokie—smoked haddock in a mild mustard sauce topped with melted cheese and served with salad and crusty bread. The à la carte menu, Tuesday–Saturday 6.30–9.30, Sunday and Monday 7–9 includes dishes such as lamb and sage cobbler, Gressingham duck breast, chicken Wellington—stuffed with herb cheese in puff pastry and the Plough mixed meat platter—steak, sausage, lamb, gammon, liver and pork. A Sunday roast is available with a choice of three meats plus a vegetarian option also four different ploughman's. A selection of sweets is offered from the blackboard. Very popular are the curry and seafood nights held on a regular basis.

Dogs welcome inside and out, children in part of the pub.

Lunchtime opening times everyday 12–2.30, Monday–Saturday evenings 6–11 Sunday 7–10.30.

Telephone: 01323 844859.

The village is signed from the A27 and the A22 west of Hailsham.

Approx. distance of walk: 3½ miles. O.S.Map. No. 199 TQ 549/096.

Park either at the pub, in Camberlot Road or in the small lay-by close to the junction in the lane opposite the school.

An enjoyable walk on field paths, through bluebell woods and on the Vanguard Way ideal for a dry summers evening or in late spring when the bluebells are at their best. Nearby Michelham Priory is a magnificent property founded in 1229 for Augustinian canons. Capturing nearly eight centuries of of history it is open daily 11 a.m. - 5.30 p.m. 25th March -31st October. Sundays only March and November 11 a.m. - 4 p.m.

1. Leave the pub turning left then left again into Camberlot Road. Further down the road take the drive on the left to Clifton Farm, bear right between the farm buildings, pass through the metal gate and climb the stile into the field on the left. Cross the field to the stile and maintain direction to the stile and bridge. Keep to the left of the ditch then cross the plank bridge and turn left through the hedge into the meadow.

2. Bearing slightly left make you way over to the stile in the far hedge and continue in the same direction where there is a wooden crossing point beside a large oak. Go into the field and across to the farm gate maintaining direction towards the ditch and the gate in the hedge beyond. Head for the barn, pass through the gate on the right and turn left through the gate onto the Vanguard Way.

3. Turn left and after about three quarter of a mile, just beyond Mount Pleasant Farm, cross the stile into the field on the left and bear half right, through the gap in the hedge and over to the stile in the far hedge. Bear left heading down the field towards the distant wood. At the finger post follow the winding path into the bluebell woods, across an area of grass and back into a smaller wood. Where a path crosses left to right keep straight ahead to the stile and continue in the same direction, cross the bridge and the stiles opposite then head up the field to the stile in the top hedge. Bear left to another stile maintaining direction across to the gate, go out into the lane, cross over and turn left back to the pub.

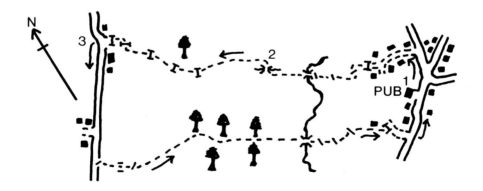

The sketch maps in this book are not necessarily to scale but have been drawn to show the maximum amount of detail.

The Greyhound, Wadhurst

The Greyhound, dating back to the 18th century, is an attractive inn very well run by the new owners, Jonathon and Emma Harrold. Described by them as a typical village local the part panelled walls in the attractive main bar make a good backdrop for the wealth of interesting regalia. A rocking chair and a comfortable padded settle are perfectly sited to warm yourself by the log fire in the large inglenook fireplace. The back section of the bar is devoted to traditional pub games like ring the bull, shove ha'penny and bar billiards. The pub also boasts a very attractive and welcoming restaurant and a pretty rear beer garden with children's play equipment

Originally owned by Bass it is now a freehouse offering a choice of real ales, which includes Bass, Harvey's Best Bitter, Old Speckled Hen plus a guest beer also a good selection of wines.

Food is served all week 12–2.30 and 7–9.30, (lunchtime only on Sunday) in the bar and restaurant. The extensive menu caters for all tastes and occasions. The menu includes moules mariniere, smoked salmon salad, Parma ham with melon followed by baked wing of skate with prawns and capers, dressed crab salad, Cajun chicken filled with Brie served with cranberry sauce and creamy mushroom pancake with cheese sauce. Sweets on offer include banoffi pie, traditional bread and butter pudding, fruit pavlova and mixed sorbets.

Well behaved children are welcome and there is no objection to dogs on a lead.

There are five charming guest rooms converted from the old stabling block. These oak-beamed rooms all have their own en-suite shower and toilet equipped to a high standard.

Weekday opening times are from 11–11. Sunday 12–10.30.

Telephone: 01892 783224. Fax: 784090. E.mail jharrold@lineone.net

Wadhurst is in the north of the county on the B2099 south east from Tunbridge Wells.

Approx. distance of walk: 4¾ miles O.S. Map No. 188 TQ 642/317.

Although the pub has a large car park you can park in the road at the front.

A lovely walk down to the very scenic Bewl Bridge Reservoir returning along peaceful lanes and on field paths.

1. From the pub cross the main road into Blacksmiths Lane opposite. When you reach the bend keep straight ahead onto the gravel track and enter the farm yard. Maintain direction towards the stile beside the gate, go over onto the track walking until you reach a pair of gates. Pass through the one on the left and continue following the track onto the grass path walking down through the trees to the stile. Keep to the narrow path and at the next stile cross over and turn right following the lake side path around the reservoir. Although a little muddy it is a very attractive walk with lovely views across the water.

2. Taking the right fork follow the path round the peninsular then round the estuary keeping close to the fence on the right until you eventually reach a finger post directing you inland. Go through the gate, up the track, over the stile and onto the driveway. Walk up past the lovely cottages and when you reach the lane turn right.

3. Follow the lane for about a quarter of a mile soon to reach a farm gate on the right, the path is signed. Keeping close to the right-hand boundary walk to the far side, go into the field ahead and turn left to pick up the track. Cross the bridge and maintain direction up to the gate, go out into the lane and turn left.

4. Upon reaching the large house on the left look for the signed footpath on the right. Go down the steps, through the gate and proceed ahead bearing left into the trees. It is well walked and easy to follow. When you reach the gate go through, cross the river and turn right, enter the field and turn left. Keeping close to the left-hand boundary walk up to the track at the top, cross to the stile opposite and turn half left following the path across the field to the stile on the far side. Go out into the main road and turn right back to the pub.

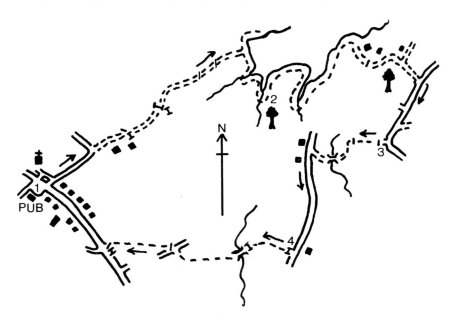

The War Bill-in-Tun, Warbleton

Hidden away in the depths of unspoilt countryside The War Bill-in-Tun occupies a peaceful spot in the centre of this very small village. The origin of the name is not known for certain but this ancient pub probably played a part in the naming of the village. The story tells of marauding soldiers intent on getting a drink tapping a barrel of beer using a battle axe. Although extensively renovated in the '70s the character of the building remains. From the small circular bar at one end steps lead down to the luxuriously furnished dining area. Deep padded, half circular seats are the norm in this cosy room, which is dominated by a massive inglenook fireplace where a log fire burns on all but the warmest of days. A few rustic seats on the small front garden are the most sought after on fine sunny days.

The inn is a freehouse owned and very well run since 1986 by Bryan and Val Whiton. Two regular real ales, dispensed by hand pump, are Harvey's Best Bitter and John Smiths Bitter plus a guest, like Friary Meux's Best Bitter.

A varied menu offers a good choice of home-cooked food all freshly prepared on the premises by Pauline. Favourite snacks include the usual ploughman's, toasted sandwiches, homemade soup, pate and jacket potatoes plus steak and kidney pie with Guinness, guinea foul, lemon sole fillets, poached salmon steak, seafood platter, pork chops and a chicken curry. Homemade sweets range from a chocolate and rum or apricot brandy gateau to a selection of exotic ice creams. A roast is served on Sunday.

Weekday opening times are from 11 till around 3 and 7–11.

Families are welcome and there is no objection to well behaved dogs on a lead.

Telephone: 01435 830636.

A difficult village to find. The most direct route is to head north from the A271 east of Hailsham to Cowbeech where the village is signed to the left.

Approx. distance of walk: 3½ miles O.S.Map No.199 TQ 609/183.

Park at the pub or in the lane.

A very enjoyable country walk across farm land, on peaceful country lanes and which follows and twice crosses an attractive stream. Whilst fairly good underfoot some areas can become muddy in the winter.

1. Turn right from the pub, enter the churchyard and make your way round to the stile in the back hedge leading into a field. Bearing slightly left walk down to the bottom, climb the bank and turn left following the line of the low electricity cables. Enter the field and make your way down to the bridge in the hedge at the bottom. Cross into the field and bear right in the direction of the waymark, up and across a second field then onto the grass track which leads round to a farm gate. Go out into the lane at Vines Cross and turn left.

2. In about half a mile turn left at the road junction and keep straight ahead at the next junction, up into the field and straight ahead walking fairly close to the hedge boundary on the right. At the bottom turn left keeping to the left hand side of the wire fence, cross the stile into the field ahead and continue round beside the hedge until you reach the stile on the right.

3. Pass through the bluebell copse and bear left. Cross the bridge and keep straight ahead, following a line fairly close to the stream on the left. After climbing the occasional stile, you will eventually reach another bridge. Cross the stream and bear right through the trees to the stile leading into the field. Maintain your direction towards the stile in the hedge then head up the field to the gates at the top. Cross the track, go through the gate into the field opposite and make your way to the stile opposite. Turn left into the drive then left again into the lane forking right at the road junction back to the pub.

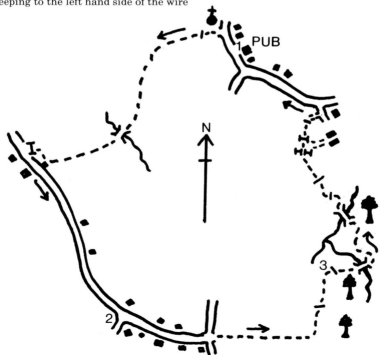

The Lamb Inn, Wartling

High above the road this attractive, white painted, two-storey inn has a small, cosy main bar with chairs beside the large open fireplace. At the other end is a large cottage-like, beamed room where a door leads off to a games room at the back. Log fires heat both bars in winter. For those wishing to dine there is a separate carvery/à la carte restaurant in a very attractive converted outhouse. There are seats outside on the small well kept front terrace.

The inn is a freehouse efficiently run by the friendly owners. Well-conditioned real ales presently available are Green King IPA plus local guest ales.

Very good food, all prepared by a qualified chef, is served every day 12–2.30 and 7–9.30. Bar snacks include tasty homemade soups like puree lentil and ham or celery and Stilton plus the usual sandwiches, ploughman's, homemade steak and kidney pie and egg and chips etc. For those wanting something more the specials boards, which are changed daily, might include baked mushrooms with garlic and herbs or homemade pate followed by grilled gammon, swordfish steaks, fresh Scottish salmon served with a smoked salmon sauce, rainbow trout filled with spinach and prawns, poached cod with a mushroom sauce, roast rack of lamb with red currant sauce and a cushion of veal in an almond and spinach sauce. For sweet lovers there is usually a choice of nine or ten ranging from millefeuille-pastry filled with cream and jam to toffee and fudge gateau. A three course carvery meal is served on Sunday.

Weekday opening times 11–3 and 6.30–11.

Families welcome, but not dogs.

Telephone: 01323 832116.

Village signed south from the A271 at Boreham Street also north from the new roundabout at the junction of the A27 and the A259.

Approx. distance of walk: 3½ miles. O.S.Map No. 199 TQ 658/092.

Park in the lane beside the pub, at the front or in the pub's own car park.

A very enjoyable walk along peaceful country lanes, through bluebell woods and across farm land passing close to the 15th century moated Herstmonceux Castle the grounds of which are open daily throughout the summer. Whilst not over demanding it can be muddy in the winter.

1. With your back to the pub walk down the lane and turn right into Boreham Lane. After about ¾ of a mile look for a stile on the left. Cross into the field and keeping close to the left-hand boundary walk round and exit into the lane on the far side. Turn left and make your way to the top of the hill.

2. Immediately before the road junction turn left onto the signed footpath into the woods keeping straight ahead at the cross track through the bluebell wood. In about 100 yards look for a path into the woods on the right, it is not well signed but the last time I was here someone had tied yellow tape to a couple of trees. Eventually when you reach the crossing point go out into the lane and walk straight across to join the signed bridleway on the right-hand side of the car park.

3. Cross the drive to the observatory and continue ahead taking care in places as the ground is well rutted and often very wet. When you reach the gate cross into the field walking only as far as the finger post then head left down to the stile. Continue walking in the direction of the arrow up to the boundary hedge following it round to the stile, climb into the field then bear left by the large oak up the rise to the stile.

4. Bear right across the field to the stile in the right-hand boundary maintaining direction to the gate beside the stile and head for the footpath to the right of the wall. Follow it round the field to the stile and along the grassy path beside the garden, over the stile onto the track and turn left up the drive to the lane then left again back to the pub.

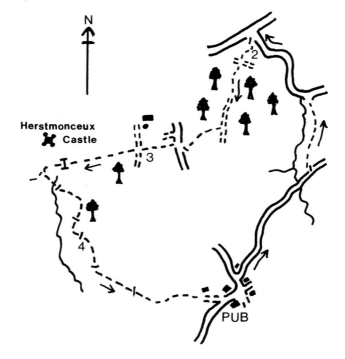

The New Inn, Winchelsea

The first town of Winchelsea was destroyed by the sea the second by its withdrawal. Built under the guidance of Edward I the streets in this ancient city were laid out to cross each other at right angles and within the squares formed, suitable plots were allocated to each householder by name. Whilst here take a little time to explore this hilltop town, to admire some of the lovely buildings, perhaps visit the museum and enjoy the views across the River Brede.

The comfortably furnished and carpeted open plan lounge bar of this impressive-looking 18th century pub has a large central fireplace housing a warm log fire in winter and is decorated with hops and old local photographs. There is a separate public bar and seating outside in the attractive orchard garden.

The well stocked bar offers a choice of real ales presently Harvey's Best Bitter and Greene King IPA.

Good home-cooked food is served every day between 12 and 2 and 6.30 (Sunday 7)–9. Daily specials such as fresh local fish, homemade steak and kidney pie, curry, Stilton and mushroom quiche and courgette, tomato and cashew bake supplement the menu, which offers a choice of eight starters and several main courses. There is a grilled leg steak of English lamb, glazed with ginger and mango, half spit roast garlic chicken, gammon steak plus breaded lobster tails, battered haddock fillets and grilled Scottish salmon fillet with hollandaise sauce. A separate Sunday lunch menu includes a couple of roasts plus a children's menu. Weekday lunchtimes only snacks like ploughman's, jacket potatoes and sandwiches.

Children welcome, dogs in garden only.

6 en-suite rooms, 4 doubles including a 4-poster, 1 twin room and 1 family room.

Opening times weekdays, 11.30–2.30 (Saturday 3) and 6.30–11, Sunday 12–3 and 7–10.30.

Telephone: 01797 226252. E.mail: newinnwsea@aol.com.

This ancient town is just off the A259 in the east of the county.

Approx. distance of walk: 4½ miles. O.S.Map No.189 TQ 904/177.

Park at the pub or anywhere in the roads around the pub.

A most enjoyable walk down to Winchelsea Beach and back across Pett Level. The going is mostly good underfoot.

1. Cross the road from the pub and walk down the lane opposite, passing the church and museum and through Strand Gate one of the ancient city gates. Turn right at the bottom of the hill into the main road walking a short distance before turning right on the road signed to Winchelsea Beach. As you reach the left-hand bend take the signed footpath on the right cutting the corner, turning right into the road again on the far side. Cross over and further ahead turn left into Willow Lane then turn right on to the track.

2. When you reach Morlais Ridge turn right following the track round to the left and keep straight ahead onto the stones then bear slightly left to join the path leading to the back gardens of the dwellings. The path then bears left across an area of gravel before turning right through a clump of trees down to meet with a track. Walk straight across onto the path leading to the

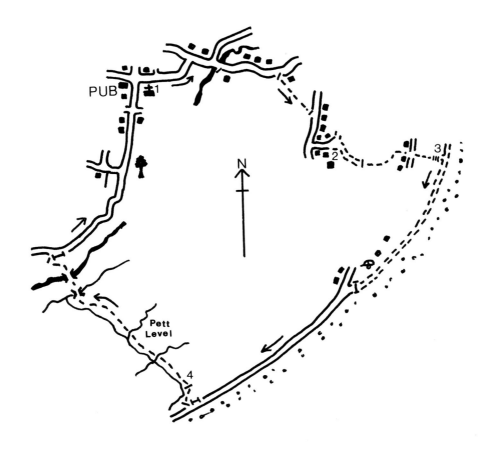

shore, cross the lane and climb the ridge turning right onto the footpath at the top.

3. There are glorious views across the beach where many wild flowers can be seen growing in the shingle. Keep walking for some distance looking for a stile in the fence on the right of the road, it is about a quarter of a mile past the point where the lane meets the road. Go over and bear right, across to a second stile then turn left following the path close to the water across Pett Level.

4. The path is easy to follow passing through a couple more gates before arriving at a concrete bridge. Cross the river and continue ahead, over the stile following the path up the rise to the stile, out into the lane and turn right. Pass under New Gate, another of the ancient city gates where it is said the French gained entry in 1380 and ransacked the town, and continue along the road turning right before the main road back to the pub.

New Gate, Winchelsea

The Swan Inn, Woods Corner (Dallington)

The simply furnished main bar of this interesting old pub, rebuilt and named in 1356 after the heraldic swan on the arms of the French king, has a low ceiling, bare boards throughout, a log burning stove in the impressive fireplace and part panelled walls upon which are hung several old photographs including pictures of the pub and the local Dallington cricket team. Windows in the dining room at the back, which boasts an interesting collection of nautical regalia, look out across the bench filled garden to the open countryside beyond. A recently built chestnut arbour seats up to 30.

The pub which, changed hands in February 2000 is now owned by Enterprise Inns and very well run as a tenanted freehouse by Gary Skipsey, the chef/proprietor who previously worked at The Star Inn, Old Heathfield. Three real ales presently available are Harvey's Best Bitter, Marston's Pedigree plus a guest.

All food served in the pub is freshly prepared to order. Served seven days a week, 12–2 and 7–9, the excellent menu, which lists the usual snacks of home-made soup, sandwiches and a dozen ploughman's, offers a range of starters/smaller portion meals such as filo wrapped prawns, fresh calamari with an anchovy dip and a sirloin steak sandwich with homemade chips. Main meals might include warm duck breast served with a hoi sin sauce and crackers, Thai green chicken curry, plus fresh dressed crab and lobster and fresh Hastings cod and chips which is available 'takeaway' Tuesday onwards from 5 pm. A speciality of the pub is 'fruits de mer' served in a Sussex trug but 36 hours notice is required. From the à la carte menu you have additional choice of sirloin steak, fresh Dover sole, lamb chops in a Provencal sauce or sautéed chicken breast served with garlic butter and cashew nuts.

Weekday opening times are from 11–3 and 5.30–11. Sunday all day 12–10.30.

Families are welcome, so too are well-behaved dogs, even muddy boots are tolerated.

Telephone: 01424 838242. E.mail:gary@theswandallington.com.

Walk No. 40

Pub on the B2096 at Woods Corner about 5 miles east of Battle.

Approx. distance of walk: 3 miles. O.S. Map No.199 TQ 667/195.

There is a good car park beside the pub, a small lay-by on the opposite side of the road and a larger one in the lane opposite.

A pretty walk which takes you through bluebell woods, along peaceful country lanes and into the lovely little village of Dallington. Whilst fairly good underfoot for most of the walk it can be a bit muddy in place during wet weather.

1. From the pub carefully cross the B2096 and follow the lane ahead towards Brightling. Keep walking until you reach the entrance on the right into Deep Park Wood. Follow the main track ahead then the next on the left. Although a fairly young wood bluebells are establishing themselves in places. Turn left at the next track, and right into the lane. Further ahead take the turning on the left to Burwash.

2. In 100 paces join the track on the left passing the recently felled bluebell wood. Upon reaching the finger post go into the field on the left and turn right making your way down to the stile at the edge of the woods. Almost immediately fork right and follow the twisting path to the stiles after which the path diverts round a fallen tree, crosses a stream and descends to a concrete driveway.

3. Turn left, pass through the gate and up the rise to the lane. Walk straight across onto the signed footpath beside the dwelling, through the gate into the field keeping close to the wire fence. Cross the stile into the adjoining field and bear right over to the stile and across the field to the crossing point on the far side. Follow the path round the edge of the wood, out on to the track by the house and continue walking until you reach a signed footpath on the left between a holly hedge and a fenced field. Walk down to the kissing gate, out into the road and turn right.

4. After passing the entrance to Brooklands cross the road and turn left towards Dallington. It is an attractive lane its hedgerows draped in summer with wild hops and honeysuckle. After a steady climb to the village pass through the churchyard or take the turning on the right to join the footpath at the back. Pass through the kissing gate and go down the field keeping close to the hedge on the right, descend the muddy bank, cross the stream climb to the stile then follow the path across the field to the gap in the hedge. Walk up to the gate on the left, go into the adjoining field and turn immediately right. Leave by the stile at the top turning left into the lane. It is just under half a mile to the pub.